Barnsley Libraries — MOBILES & HOUSEBOUND — MH

Return Date: 11/08

- 6 APR 2009
12 MAR 2009
30. NOV 09
13. OCT 11
26. SEP 12
10A
/4RS
19 JUN 2015
14RM
22 APR
MDR
30 NOV 2018

JW(L@L)
19 JAN 2021
3AW
11 MAR 2021
DY11
5 - MAY 2021
9C
14 JUL 2021
7M.S
- 7 OCT 2021
13 BH
15 MAR 2022
12 APR 2022
TAN

All for Barnsley

Mel Dyke

Wharncliffe Publishing

For My Family
Lest They Forget

First Published in 2003 by
Wharncliffe Books
an imprint of
Pen and Sword Books Limited,
47 Church Street, Barnsley,
South Yorkshire. S70 2AS

Copyright © Mel Dyke 2003

For up-to-date information on other titles produced under the Wharncliffe imprint, please telephone or write to:

**Wharncliffe Books
FREEPOST
47 Church Street
Barnsley
South Yorkshire S70 2BR
Telephone (24 hours): 01226 734555**

ISBN: 1-903425-49-2 paperback
1-903425-52-2 hardback

All rights reserved. No part of this publication may be reproduced, stored in a retrieval system, or transmitted, in any form or by any means, electronic, mechanical, photocopying, recording or otherwise, without the prior permission in writing of the publishers.

This book is sold subject to the condition that it shall not, by way of trade or otherwise, be lent, resold, hired out or otherwise circulated without the publisher's prior consent in any form of binding or cover other than that in which it is published and without a similar condition including this condition being imposed on the subsequent purchaser.

A CIP catalogue record of this book is available from the British Library

Printed in the United Kingdom by
CPI UK

Contents

Stan Richards	11
Kenny Doughty	18
David Markwell	24
Jenni Murray	27
Jane Sanderson	32
Philip Mosley	37
Mick McCarthy	42
Dickie Bird	48
Geoffrey Boycott	55
David Sugden	63
Joan Booth	68
Joanne Harris	72
Arthur Scargill	76
Joyce Winsett	84
Hedley Salt	88
Lord Mason	91
Martin Brook	96
Ashley Jackson	101
Sir Thomas Elmhirst	109
Rita Britton	120
Ronnie Dukes and Ricki Lee	134
Susan Wolff	137
Romilly Mullen	143
Josh Wood	146
The Calendar Girls	149

Foreword

In one of his essays about his Yorkshire boyhood, Roy Hattersley has this to say: 'As a youth I had one unique attribute. I believed there was something tender and romantic about Barnsley.' It took a Sheffield man to write that, and I do believe that we can indeed find something almost alluring in a place very much like our own but *somewhere else*.

Barnsley imprinted itself on my consciousness way back between the two world wars. My father had relatives in Darton and, visiting them one time, we took a trip into Barnsley. They met someone they knew. It was after dark and while they chatted I, no more than six or seven, stood in the blaze of light from the corner window of a jeweller's shop, while people passed to and fro. Why something as trivial as that should have lingered in my imagination for nearly seventy years I really do not know; but I can tell you that the lights of the 'big city' never shone with such mystery and magic again.

Just after World War Two I used to visit a friend who lived in Mapplewell (or was it Staincross? I never worked out the difference). We were not given to getting drunk and shouting in the streets but we got quiet enjoyment from an evening at one or other of Barnsley's cinemas (I particularly remember the splendour of the Ritz) followed by dancing at the Cuban Ballroom, over a row of shops in the town centre. If we bussed in, ten to one we walked home afterwards, (it was downhill going that way.) There may, by that time, have been something already stirring in me which would later lead me to try to write, but I surely could not have known that by the late 70s and early 80s I should be speaking to audiences of a hundred and more at meetings, in the Central Library, of one of the most vigorous literary societies I have ever known.

'Where there's muck there's brass,' they used to say. Aye, an' happen there's summat else an' all – more talent than you can shake a stick at. Mel Dyke loves talent. She loves people who *do* things. She herself is a great 'doer', a mover, a maker of things to happen, particularly in the world of Barnsley education and the areas and activities on which it impinges and which it energises.

We first met when she invited me to a dramatic entertainment fashioned by her pupils out of the hearing into the death by drowning of children in the Silkstone pit disaster, in the 1840s. This led to a prize-giving on the eve of closure of her then school, and some years later, a request that I help in the recording of witness by the people of Grimethorpe when Michael Heseltine dealt coal-mining its final blow.

I have set out to show my longstanding respect and affection for Barnsley and its people, but I am, all the same, quite staggered by the roster of native talent assembled by Mel Dyke in these fascinating profiles. It being Barnsley, much of the achievement celebrated had its roots in the humblest of beginnings, and is all the more satisfying because of that.

As one of Mel's subjects, Ashley Jackson, says here: 'When you think you can't do something all you have to do is get off your arse and make the effort and you'll find you can do it!'

Well, not entirely and not for everybody. But it's that positive attitude which drives everything in this book and which makes me more than proud to contribute this foreword.

Stan Barstow.

Stan Barstow.

Stan Barstow agreed to write other peoples' words to help produce the Book in a Day at Grimethorpe on October 24th 1992, with the author, and local MP for Barnsley Central, Eric Illsley. *Author's collection*

Introduction

I never felt I could take to Oliver Cromwell. There was nothing of the Che Guevara, Robin Hood or even Guy Fawkes in him for my money. Then there was that wart, which I am certain periodically obscured his view. It must have done the day he visited the ancient priory at Monk Bretton since he announced, 'This land is of little worth.' Whether the story is apocryphal or not, like my view of Cromwell, is irrelevant. What is a fact is that the road to Monk Bretton is called Littleworth Lane, and a notion that Barnsley is unworthy of serious recognition prevails to this day. It is one of those places that manages to be the butt of jokes, without even trying.

Its former image, as a dirty coal town, concealed a quality, Barnsley coal was burned in the finest houses in the country, including Buckingham Palace and No. 10 Downing Street. Glass-blowing, another historic industry here is reflected not just in the town's crest, but in the transparently unpretentious character of its people and its motto *Spectemur Agendo*, by our deeds we are known. The traditional directness, or bluntness, is often translated as confrontational, or lacking in social grace. It should be remembered however that Donald Davie, author of *The Purity of Diction in English Verse*, and *Articulate Energy* was born and educated in Barnsley, as was Alexander Pope's mother.

The town is set in beautiful scenery, loved by those of us who choose to live here. Our problem is that some tend to see only Barnsley's warts, in the way I do Cromwell's.

The best of Barnsley is the people, without a doubt. FA Premier League Chief Executive, Richard Scudamore, wrote to schoolchildren here after Barnsley FC's failure to regain Premier Division status, calling the town, and the people remarkable. He exhorted them to be proud to belong to a town which made friends of almost the entire football playing, managing and supporting world, with a team that gained the respect of the nation whilst playing the game fairly and giving their best.

The Red Sea for the last play-off at Wembley Stadium against Ipswich 2000. *The author*

But it's not just football, coal and directness that the town should be famous for. Hewn from the bedrock for generations is a seam of ability, effort, talent and initiative that has led to some remarkable achievements. It was a wine-bar debate a year or two ago that led a young solicitor in Sutton Coldfield to concede defeat after trying to match local achievers there against Barnsley's. His view, that the town's image belied its real accomplishment, led to this book. It is a wart-free celebration of just some of those achievements, in an attempt to redress the balance of outsiders' perceptions. Quite deliberately there are no weakest links and no intentional criticism of any view held, except for Oliver Cromwell that is.

Included here are those I have been able to meet and who have agreed to help. Many were reluctant, in part because they underestimate their own accomplishment, but also because they are wary of comparisons by those who feel others should have been included. Clearly the list is shorter than it could be due to the level of talent, and the wide range across which it is spread. Television, theatre, cinema, sport, local and national radio, ballet, football, cricket, education, writing, trade unionism, politics, entrepreneurialism, art, fashion, design, hairdressing and charity fund-raising are only the first considerations with as many projected for a second volume. Predictably the list will increase with other suggestions by other people.

All those who have co-operated in the project did it to motivate the next generation of achievers from Barnsley. They were for me a fascinatingly diverse group with a variety of backgrounds, dreams, ambitions, spurs, obstacles and talents, but had one thing in common. They all believe Barnsley grit helped them realise their aims and objectives, whether they were born Barnsley, became it, or simply had it thrust upon them, they are all for Barnsley.

Special Acknowledgements

My heartfelt thanks go to:

The man whose writing I have admired and taught all my working life. His vivid representation of characters in towns like Barnsley is so real it can only be born of belonging, and a kind of loving. Stan Barstow makes writers out of readers.

All staff at Wharncliffe Publication have done more than I could have expected, even from a team strong in local support and professional integrity as they are.

John Britton freely gave time, effort and professional expertise to illustrate the publication supported by advice and encouragement from Terry Logan.

Margaret Trott typed the majority of drafts and re-drafts speedily and energetically. For the final drafts I am eternally indebted to my ever trusty friend, who insists on taking no credit.

My son Tim shared his professional expertise and advice, and my daughter Stephanie Watson tirelessly and patiently proofread every word with lucid insight, and occasionally ruthless editing, to improve what I had lost the ability to see for myself.

1
Stan Richards

Actor, Comedian, Musician

Ask anyone to identify who would be listed in *TV legends – The World's Top Ten Kings of Soaps*, and you might well expect them to include Larry Hagman, more famous as J R Ewing, from Dallas. You probably would not expect to find, four places above him on the list, one Stanley Richardson a former clerk in an office of the Civil Service in Barnsley, but he was. You might be totally gobsmacked to hear that this septuagenarian then went on to become an official pin-up. Not only was he chosen by Wrens serving on *HMS Ark Royal*, but also by the male ratings on the helicopter carrier *HMS Ocean*. 'I was amused but flattered and thrilled to be asked by the girls, but not too sure about those lads on 'The Ocean', says the man himself, aka Stan Richards, musician, comedian and actor, but best known as Seth from Emmerdale. As Stan says, 'I'm a bit like Madonna aren't I? I'm known best by just one name that isn't mine!'

Stan's stage career actually started at the age of ten, when his father invested £40 in a piano for his son to learn to play. A small fortune in those days, and as Stan's mother remarked with pride, 'There's only two pianos in our street and that's one of them.' Church Choirmaster, Mr Charles Harrison, began the tuition and young Stanley quickly grasped the rudiments and learned to play *Home Sweet Home*. Despite it being the only piece he could play, his father proudly took him to Gawber Working Men's Club and introduced him as a genius. Technically that was also Stan's first paid appearance as the steward pulled his Dad a free pint whilst they listened to the protégé play. He pulled a second and a third following Mr Richardson's calls for encores. 'Well done Stanley,' said Mr Richardson as they went home, both happy, Stanley with his first public success and father with his new found liquid asset. Stanley soon extended his range to include Bach and Mozart but much preferred Fats Waller's *Alligator Crawl* and Hoagy Carmichael's *Skylark*. He was strongly influenced by the then popular Charlie Kunz, developing a powerful left hand, which is still evident in his playing today. He regards the next stage in his tuition as a major factor in that skill. He was taught to play the piano accordion, with its dependence on left-hand dexterity by another Barnsley success, Horace Crossland, who was World Amateur Champion Accordion player. Pearl Fawcett of Barnsley also won similar acclaim in the early 1960s.

Gradually combining his strengths, improvising and, introducing tenths and inverted tenths into his practice, he would counter piano teacher Mr Harrison's purist reservations, by persuading him that the pieces had been improved by his additions. By the time he was fifteen he was playing piano in local dance bands at night, whilst attending Holgate Grammar School during the day. He joined *The Ambassadors* and played at Barnsley Baths during the winter months when the pool was covered over with a dance floor – reckoned to be the best-sprung in the North of England. He became a favourite in pubs in the town, including the then sophisticated, now demolished, *Three Cranes Hotel*, where he played with the *Rhythm Aces* until he nearly got the sack for 'acting daft.'

The oddball sense of humour, however, fitted the *Melody Maniacs* with whom he played the club circuit, miming to *Cocktails for Two* by the then fashionable Spike Jones and his City Slickers, and other zany numbers. The 'acting daft' developed into a stand-up comedy routine. In this Stan was inspired and influenced by one of his great comedy heroes, another Barnsley boy, Albert Modley. Better than most, Modley hid his wit and talent behind a façade of 'gormlessness', rivalling George Formby and arguably out-playing him as a naïve Northerner in the wonderful 1930s film send-up *Up for the Cup*. In stage performances Modley appeared incredibly versatile as he interwove his comedy act, apparently playing a wide range of musical instruments confidently. Stan reveals the secret: Modley had actually learned to play only one tune on each instrument, but no one guessed. He was a master of understated self-deprecation, which, combined with a little baiting, is an essential element of that brand of humour known in Barnsley as slow-timing. He would tell stories of 'two Barnsley lads' in the vein that others were telling topical Englishman, Irishman, Scotsman or German jokes and rejoice in his catch-phrase: 'In't it great when you're barmy?'

Barmy he wasn't, he was shrewd enough to succeed in a cut-throat business in an impoverished era. Stan reveres this talent as greatly today as when it first influenced and motivated him. You couldn't fail to spot similarities in his characterisation of Seth – who is never quite defeated. *Brewer's Dictionary of Phrase and Fable* quotes a Yorkshire farmer under cross-examination being baited by a lawyer who asked if there were still as many fools as ever in the West Riding. Apparently subdued, the farmer replied, 'Well, no sir. We've got our fair

Albert Modley back in Barnsley at the Theatre Royal. *The author's collection*

share, no doubt, but there are not quite as many as when you were last there!' For the benefit of the uninitiated, that is slow timing.

The apparent fall and rise of the 'working-class twerp' as opposed to the 'upper-class twit' mirrored the shifting class development as educational influences affected perspectives, tastes, aspirations and expectations throughout the Twentieth century. From stage, radio, screen and TV, though not necessarily in that order, Stan's favourite duo, Morecambe and Wise, had grown. Morecambe's original gormless start through to a sophisticated black-tie finale is an example of the growing possibility of switching from twerp to twit and back with ease and without question.

Stan's other heroes died as tragically early as Eric Morecambe, Tommy Cooper and The Goons. Only the genius of Ken Dodd for him, and for me, remains as a living exponent of the art. Like Doddy, Stan has used his appearance to his advantage. Dodd's teeth and mad hairstyle in combination with his introduction of himself as 'failed accountant and male model' flag up from the start that you laugh with him – not at him.

The indefatigable Kenneth Arthur Dodd, finishing a five-hour stint on stage. One of his earliest appearances was at Barnsley's Theatre Royal fifty years ago. The author

Stan has the enormous moustache and has for years signed photographs for fans like my daughter Stephanie, who still has the photo some thirty years later, and now lays claim to having started the surreal pin-up trend. His autograph to her read, 'You'll notice I'm tall and dark. Two out of three's not bad, is it?'. That moustache is now contracted, insured and rated as a top Yorkshire tourist attraction.

He learned the discipline of the stage as a boy, enthralled by that cavalcade of legendary performers at the old style theatres like the Theatre Royal. He loves to reminisce and has an encyclopaedic store of anecdotes gleaned in his years in the business. He reminds me of first and last performances on a stage in Barnsley. Arthur Lucan's wife, Kitty McShane, had left him leaving little prospect of him using the act for which they had both become famous, old Mother Riley and her daughter Kitty. He now did a shorter act based on the old song *On Mother Kelly's Doorstep*. On his last night in Barnsley, the tired, fading and ageing comic actor was too ill to perform and Stan recalls watching him from the audience just sitting on stage whilst the chorus team took over the singing. The following night, Arthur Lucan died before going on stage in a theatre in Hull.

Having witnessed the end of one famous music hall career, the theatre was the starting point of another. The BBC wireless programme *A Seat in the Circle* was recorded in a different theatre across the country each week. The week it was recorded in Barnsley, the bottom of the bill was a young and unknown Irish tenor who became an overnight sensation. Joseph Locke was made a star, and a generation of eighteen year old boys went off to do their National Service strengthened by his rendition of *A Soldier's Dream – See Them Pass By*. Their mothers in contrast, were first reduced to tears by the *Goodbye* chorus, and subsequently seduced back into swaying rhythmic acceptance as they Monday washed and ironed singing along to *Hear My Song, Violetta*. Locke remained a big favourite in the town which had come to regard him as one of it's own and went on to support him when he was forced into exile by tax demands. It was common place to hear locals asking where Mr X was appearing, and if he had sung the old favourites on his 'secret' re-appearances to play clubs and theatres under that assumed name for years after, in one of the worst – kept secrets in stage history. Like most families in the area, the Richardson's annual week's holiday would be in Blackpool. They would book theatre tickets in advance by tuppenny post, ensuring good first house seats every night at the Palace of Varieties, Feldman's, The Hippodrome, The Opera House, all three piers and one matinee performance at the Tower Circus. One of Stan's treasured memories from those days is going to the Hippodrome on one occasion and seeing Canadian couple Ted and Barbara Andrews bring on stage their ten year old daughter to sing. Little Julie Andrews brought the house down and stole the show with her rendition of *The Miller's Daughter* and *One Fine Day*. As big a hit some fifty years later as *Mary Poppins* delighting my granddaughters Amelia and India, they share Stan's view that she is still amazing.

He recalls another Barnsley man Harry Worth. You need only mention the name to be guaranteed a ridiculous response from otherwise normal men and women of a certain age. They will stand on one leg, raising the other leg and one arm. This is silent homage to Harry Worth's famous corner shop window trick of vertical levitation. Like Stan, he recalls, Harry Worth started very young and as a budding ventriloquist gave performances for other kids in the back yard of his home in Pilley, charging them one old penny for a Saturday afternoon show. Equally loved is Charlie Williams, still living in the town though no longer well enough to perform his gently satirical and fiercely funny act from *The Comedians* innovatively debunking prejudice in every form.

On his way to the top via the pubs in Barnsley, Stan lost his job as one of *The Four Renowns* and was thrown into a solo situation, which proved to be his big break. He soon became 'Comedian of the Year' and found

Emmerdale Stars Seth and Smokey. *Emmerdale Press Office Yorkshire Television*

himself in demand for appearances in the newly blossoming club-land scene. The Fiesta in Sheffield, The Chesterfield Aquarius, Barnsley's Club BaBa, The Wakefield Theatre Club and Batley Variety Club had him playing solo as a pianist with a comedy act or, a comic who played the piano. He was even Sacha Distel's warm-up man. He worked on the same bills as some of the greatest names in show business. Eventually, he was offered a part in Barry Hines' *The Price of Coal*, working with Ken Loach, who sought out local talent. Fast to follow were appearances in films and TV, including *Crown Court, All Creatures Great and Small, Last of The Summer Wine*, more than a dozen TV commercials, and, of course, *Coronation Street*. He even got a month's contract on a TV series called *Emmerdale Farm*, and was an overnight success. Playing Seth Armstrong, he is now the longest serving member of the cast of any British TV soap, with the exception of *Coronation Street*. His own dog, Smokey, was Barnsley's first small screen rival to Lassie when he was given a part in Emmerdale without an audition. It was agreed that having accompanied Stan on set frequently he demonstrated more natural flair and obedience than some of the prima donna professional contenders for the part.

As Stan looks back over his life it is clear he has worked with some of the best performers and directors in the business, but cannot believe it. He still looks slightly bemused when asked to identify his favourite memory. Apart from being the subject of *This is Your Life* in 1991, he includes discussing the development of his role in *Agatha* whilst filming with Dustin Hoffman and Vanessa Redgrave. 'You couldn't make it up,' he muses.

The lows of screen acting for him, include the long waits between takes and re-takes, together with the occasional actor who arrives unprepared. 'Not professional conduct,' says the longest-serving member of the *Emmerdale* cast. That is advice he would give to aspiring young actors: 'Learn your lines, know everybody else's in the script and then concentrate on being directed. If you are lucky enough to work with someone who is strong in artistic direction, you will be amazed how much you will learn.' Stan believes that the rewards for all the effort required to achieve success in the rough and competitive world of entertainment are worth the hard work. It can mean achieving a life-long ambition, meeting amazing people, earning a living whilst living the dream; and sometimes if you have both talent and luck, and work at it, winning fame and accolades along the way. He copes well with the interruptions of people asking for autographs and reminding him they knew him briefly forty seven or twenty two years ago, when they travelled on the same bus, or used the same butcher.

It would be impossible to remember everyone, but he does well and manages to look as if he does remember them all. What he certainly never forgot were his roots and the early years of observing, rehearsing, adapting, refining and always learning. He stored experience to improve his performance in similar fashion to Ken Dodd who still keeps a record of what material he has used, where, when and how it was received. Stan too found that kind of information useful, invited by Jim Davison and Jim Bowen to take part in a Charity Show in Blackpool. He found to his dismay that the act before him, Scorch the Dragon, had reduced the audience of three and a half thousand to total hysteria. He was expected to follow it with a serious performance of *Tchaikovsky's Piano Concerto No. 1*. He knew it did not bode well. Formally, he made his way to the grand piano, took his seat and with a dramatic flourish began to pound out the opening chords. On reaching the end of the keyboard, he continued in a frenzy of fingers and fell flat on his face as he ran out of piano. Quickly back on his feet, he complained loudly to stage left that he had been promised a longer piano when the same thing had happened on a previous visit. The audience loved it and went along happily with the classical change of pace. The Melody Maniac was back.

After playing Seth for more than a quarter of a century, Stan Richards is a contented man and a satisfied professional. He feels no pressure except that of giving his best at every performance. 'It's become so easy now,' he says. 'When I put that cap on, I am Seth. I don't see a camera or a mike.' Only once in our talk did Stan look surprised by a question. I asked why he had stayed in Barnsley. 'It's my home,' he said, pointing to a window in the pub that is his Barnsley local. 'That's where I used to come every night as a kid to the off-sales to get three gills of ale in a jug for my Dad. My whole family either lives here or is buried in the churchyard here, so my heart's here'.

Quickly recovering, Stan Richardson slots in the last quip, 'And I've no need to move now, I think I've learned the secret of acting – it's total sincerity! Learn how to fake that and the rest is a cinch.' With that he sits at the piano and as deftly as ever plays Hoagy Carmichael, winking occasionally to flag up for me when a tenth was inverted.

2
Kenny Doughty

Actor

The first time I can remember watching Kenny Doughty on a stage, he was eleven years old, and I was producing *Children of the Dark* at The Oaks School in Kendray. Head of English Dick Walker, who was directing and providing the music for the production, asked me to watch a group of boys audition for speaking parts. They were all good, but this one was different. Clearly nervous to begin with, he climbed onto the high stage, and confidently delivered the poignant speech he had learned by heart; and then showed his real potential. He smiled. It was not simply the smile of relief because he had completed the audition without hesitation or error. We knew it was an implicit signal that he understood that despite working like men, underground for twelve or fourteen hours

Kenny Doughty's first public performance with staff and other pupils in the *Children of the Dark* at the Oaks School, Kendray 1987. *The author*

Children of the Dark dress rehearsal with Head of Biology Charles Lowery next to Kenny Doughty and other pupils. *The author's collection*

a day, these were still children, and that the smile would show that to the audience.

His memory of the production remains equally strong. Performed first in the school for mining families, parents and a range of educationalists, it was then taken to the church at the scene of the tragedy it portrayed, at the invitation of the Reverend Derek Birch, then Vicar of Silkstone. Doughty recalls the atmospheric stillness, the silence of the audience, broken only by muffled sobbing from the audience reliving a tragedy that killed twenty six children who were forced to earn a living. It was his first public appearance and not only he was moved by it. Author Stan Barstow, The Lord Mason of Barnsley and the local members of Parliament applauded the children's interpretations, and the media gave it unqualified praise. Kenny Doughty recalls a sense of pride re-inforcing his keen wish to act.

At fifteen he was in a new school and a new genre, dancing and singing in The Kingstone School's production of *Grease*. He found this daunting since he felt singing was not his forte, but was still looking for a way into acting professionally. An advertisement in *The Barnsley Chronicle* inviting young people to audition for the National Youth Theatre, caught his eye. Acceptance led him to a six-week stay in Manchester, with dozens of like minded youngsters under the guidance of professional directors and crew. It was the turning point in his life.

Despite being advised by his new mentors that life for an actor is full of pitfalls, he knew that whatever the cost, it was going to be his life from now on. He decided then that intermittent poverty, the long periods of unemployment, and filling those gaps between acting parts doing any job that would earn a crust, were the price he would pay to live his dream. It totally defied the careers advice he had been given, 'Acting is a hobby, think about a real career, like journalism'. Disregarding the advice totally, he opted to follow his own belief in himself. This was raised to a new level by the Director at Manchester, Paul Janes, who told him, 'You have an enormous talent, and I'm not going to let you waste it'. His mother, Julie Saunders had had total faith in his ability and potential since he was small, and she told him she would support whatever he honestly felt he could do well.

For three years he committed himself to a self imposed, intensive programme. Studying for 'A' levels in Psychology, English Literature and Theatre Studies, he also returned to Manchester each summer to absorb more of their expertise and support, whilst additionally working on a voluntary basis at West Yorkshire Playhouse. His goal was to get to know as much as possible about every aspect of the acting industry. His strategy was a sound combination of hands on practical experience and tuition, and academic theory. Of those days he says, 'I had not only a dream to fulfil, but a purpose in life, and I was learning to believe in myself. I just felt that with perseverance, and enough hard work, I could make it happen'.

With his 'A' levels came a tutor's opinion that he would never be an actor. He received it in the same manner he had the careers advice, three years earlier. He sensed in himself a new strength, that if anyone told him he could not do it, he would have to prove them wrong. He remembered Paul Janes' words and also the confidence of family friend and mentor Jim Ebbage, whose gift of a book led him to Stanislowski and further inspiration. There was also his mother's unfailing encouragement and emotional support. He took this as a debt of gratitude that he had to repay with success. He applied to five drama schools in London, at a fee of £25 per audition, and was turned down by all of them. Naturally disappointed, he accepted the judgement that his voice had not matured sufficiently. His disappointment was lessened when he was asked to return for a free audition in a year's time. The year could not be wasted, he firmly believes that life and time are too precious to waste. He researched the market, put together a business plan, got himself onto a Government Young Enterprise Scheme, and set up his own touring theatre company. He had clearly learned the art of compromise.

He wasted no opportunity, travel enabled him to listen carefully to a range of accents and dialects; and add them to his growing repertoire. 'It's fairly easy once you learn a few new vowels sounds, the trick, I believe is not to imitate or parody, it's to listen to the music, then own the music.

Being from Barnsley was never an issue for me, nobody was ever judgmental about my accent in the early days. But it did help in taking hard knocks, nobody there would tolerate you staying down if you got knocked down. You were expected to get up stronger, start again, readier next time to face adversity. That is a help in this business. It doesn't matter if the big break doesn't come for me, being rich and famous isn't my goal. Being my best is, I just love acting'.

He says he has experienced the ultimate in acting, being taught once by Sir Alec Guiness, 'He said so little, he seemed to make no effort, he just did it, and it happened. We asked him all kinds of questions he couldn't answer, he said he couldn't explain acting, he could only do it. He was a phenomenon, a legend, and I spent half a day watching him'.

A year later and he was back on the audition circuit, mature in more than voice. This time he received three offers of places. His deliberation was as meticulously considered as his previous year had been planned. His choice, The Guildhall School of Music and Drama was based on his individual needs, style and personality.

He regards himself fortunate to have received a major educational award, which covered the fees of the course. There was, however, the high cost of living in London for the next three years. For the first time he felt he had encountered a hurdle that he could not clear. It was more daunting than any of the negative advice he had been given, then he had an amazing stroke of luck. A visit to Hardwick Hall, with his mother and aunt led to a chance meeting with an American. A successful economist, and previous advisor to the then President Clinton, he was an Ivy League graduate who now identified potential in young people who in his view, warranted support to develop it. With no strings, Kenny Doughty became one of many who were to benefit from the generosity and sponsorship of the unnamed philanthropist.

At Guildhall he met tutorial expertise, leadership and support on a level he had not thought existed, in the form of Chattie Salamon. He was instantly at ease with both her amazing sense of humour, and her total intolerance of unprofessional behaviour. He felt she was the established existence of a philosophy that would perfectly develop his own emergent one. 'She taught me more than I thought I could learn,' he muses. 'She taught us that accepting failure led to leaping forward. She pushed us constantly, further and further to explore and discover. Just when we thought we were there, she would say, 'You need to know you will never be as good as Olivier!' God she was brilliant.'

He left the course with a BA Hons in Drama and felt skilled and equipped to be an actor. It quickly became clear that style, dialect, looks, attitude, stamina and the determination to push forward were required too. These are frequently in the eye of the beholder, and the beholder spotted his suitability for a lead role in a BBC production *Anorak of Fire*. There he was given more sound advice from the Director. 'The parts you turn down are just as important as the parts you accept in making you a success'. 'It's good advice, but it isn't easy to turn down work when you're on the breadline. It taught me though, you should never sell your soul. You should have values and always hold on to them. Keeping your spirits up is important too, it's difficult not to become depressed by inappropriate scripts, or even worse, no scripts. You have to strike a balance, to look for scripts that offer creativity and integrity, but I'm not stupid enough to starve for a dream. You have to keep looking, reading, auditioning, pushing until something comes along. Then it's all worth it. But nobody is going to hand it to you, you have to scrap for your dreams'.

What has come along for him is a wide, wonderful range of parts to enjoy and be stretched by. Early appearances in *Heartbeat* and *Dinner Ladies* and live theatre in Noel Coward's *Present Laughter* in Manchester and an adaptation of a Turgenev book in Prague. American television film parts, then playing alongside some of the greatest established names in the business, Lord Attenborough in *Elizabeth* with Geoffrey Rush and Christopher Eccleston, and as Sir Anthony Hopkins' son in *Titus*. 'Filming in Rome, and watching and learning from greats like Sir Anthony and Jessica Lange, just amazing, he is such a complex craftsman, just observing him lifted me to new heights'. The sexy male lead with Andie McDowell in *Crush* followed and put him in the heart throb league.

If you have already seen *Crush*, you will realise that it was not removing his clothes that led his next producer to provide a nutritionist, and ask him to lose one and a half stones for his next film. Joining Joseph Fiennes, Ben Bratt and James Franco in Australia, he plays a World War Two prisoner of war in *The Great Raid*, due for release in February 2004. A completely new experience, making a big Hollywood movie, but one he has enjoyed.

Kenny Doughty taking a rare break from filming.
The author

The BBC's 2003 series, a modern day adaption of Chaucer's legendary *Canterbury Tales*, features him in *The Miller's Tale* with James Nesbitt and Denis Waterman, 'a bit of a legend himself.' Next in line is a return to Yorkshire to work with ex-Bretton Hall student, and author, Kay Mellor, in her latest TV film *Gifted*. The rush of work, from the good parts now on offer, validate Doughty's philosophy of screening and refusing to compromise his standards. It leaves little time for relaxation, but a break from her long-term work in *Holby City*, for his fiancée Caroline Carver, allows time together.

I watched him last when in Holland to interview another Barnsley winner, Professor Joan Booth. BBC reception was good so I did not have to miss the fifth episode of Lucy Gannon's *Servants*, which had been compulsive viewing for me for the previous month. Vying with Joe Absalom for girls and for promotion, Doughty portrayed William Forrest as crude, gullible, lascivious, immoral, shiftless and lacking integrity, the complete opposite of Doughty himself. When I ask him if he prefers one role to another, or being a heart-throb, he quotes Vasilly Skorik, on love, art and passion. 'Truth and reality have no link with believability'. Then he gives what is more than a smile, it is a big grin.

3

David Markwell

Programme Editor and Producer BBC Radio Sheffield

When he was nine years old, he wanted to be Noel Edmunds, or at least the star of the *Radio One Road Show*. He imagined himself on radio, performing live, mixing, fading and creating new sounds with revolutionary intros and links. Lots of kids do before moving on to be the greatest footballer in the world or whatever the next fantasy happens to be.

Not David Markwell though. After years of practice with a spoon for a microphone, then transforming his parents' Dansette record player into his own imaginary radio studio, he got himself a job. At fourteen he became a voluntary contributor to Barnsley's Hospital Radio Station. Feeling that he had never experienced any success at school he compensated by absorbing himself in a world of sound. The lack of early fulfilment faded as he began to develop skills in the medium that led him to his first real job at sixteen, unsurprisingly in the local record shop, Playback.

His grandfather, Herbert Cawthorne, was a member of the Magic Circle and the youngster was encouraged by him to believe that he really could have a future in the world of entertainment. From him he learned how to perform tricks, do sleight of hand and most importantly, how to gauge an audience. From him too he learned to enjoy and understand that there was fun as well as potential value in collecting. In his case it was unusual records, foreign tracks, TV themes and the comedy of the spoken-word. They became a passion that made retention and interlinking a simple operation. Committed to his memory is an ever-growing encyclopaedic knowledge of old radio programmes, records and comedy links.

By a stroke of luck he spotted an advertisement in a local newspaper for applications from people interested in joining a funded development of Performing Arts in Barnsley. The project led him and subsequently hundreds of others to Chris Evans, the director who encouraged him to use all his stored knowledge, and to develop new skills and direction. Doors began to open that he had never anticipated and he was thrilled to be part of a workshop with the Royal Shakespeare Company's visit to the town. For the first time in his life he felt the pulsation of working alongside top ranking professionals. He was inspired by daily involvement in watching and learning from Daniel Day Lewis and Sheila Hancock, which fired the latent talent and early ambition in the youngster. He could not believe that he was doing something he loved, whilst feeling a sense of achievement and having the amazing opportunity of watching and learning from someone like Trevor Nunn.

When a full-time vacancy for a technician arose with the Electric Light Theatre Company, he applied and was offered the post. Even though it meant turning down an offer to join a Theatre, Stage and Film-making course at Rose Bruford College in Kent, he accepted the offer, which gave him freedom to work with the company's extensive range of technology and equipment whilst allowing him to continue developing his own style. It seemed his granddad might have been right, he might have a magic touch. It was less visual though than auditory. What he had always felt was inadequacy, his lack of academic success, gradually diminished by the emergence of these other skills, far more relevant to his chosen career. He possessed a natural ability to think laterally reflected in the ease with which he could transform any sound signal problem from A to B or C or D. This combination, together with his initiative strengthened his determination and he applied for a job with BBC Radio Sheffield. He rates determination highly on the list of pre-requisites for success in radio, 'especially if you have a Barnsley accent you intend to keep'.

He is comfortable with the accent and the dialect. It is re-assuring to hear a young voice preserving Viking influence in contrast with the Norman invasion of the language. It is good to know too that he implicitly acknowledges that fettling is as much a Northern trait as tholing, and here gormlessness, originally meant not to heed rather than to appear stupid – an intention not a disability. He could not bring himself to admit to finesse, but he has it, together with a typically local dismissal of veneer or 'side'. He also has a universal appeal, much of which is innate but some acquired during his next assignment.

Promotion to producer brought him into contact with local legend and world-famous-round-here lover in the afternoon, Tony Capstick. Their relationship spontaneously developed into an on-air partnership that made them arguably the funniest team on recent radio. With daily performances that ran the gamut of comedy from acerbic to zany they made local radio compulsory listening five afternoons a week. Mutual respect and admiration was deftly concealed by wit, banter and argument that ranged from surreal nonsense to colloquial slow-timing of each other and also of the listening audience. Frequently caustic, even raucous but never vulgar or vindictive, their exchanges ranged from the benign to out-raged irritation, the upper-hand passing from one to the other with spontaneous ease.

Markwell had accidentally become the performer his grandfather had predicted years earlier, and was now meeting people he had hero-worshipped in the days of the Dansette Radio Shows. He could not believe that he was to do a programme with *The Crickets*, who, backing the greatest Buddy Holly, had been amongst his favourites. He is one of the few young people I know who would instantly recognise that Peanuts Hucko was lead clarinet with the legendary Glen Miller Orchestra when he visited Radio Sheffield.

His granddad is still his hero, but that he rates the ability and integrity of Mick McCarthy and admires Ian Macmillan, the poet laureate of Barnsley whom he regards as a clever, clever, clever man. No mention now of Noel Edmunds! Working with the acting greats like Daniel Day Lewis were experiences he had not planned in life, but little of his career has been planned. His move to Programme Editor at Radio Sheffield leaves those of us who could not drive a car in the afternoons without occasionally pulling in to the roadside to finish laughing in safety at the latest exchange between him and Cappo, totally bereft as the show finished. It does however allow his individuality and flair across the full range of programme provision and also led to the introduction of upwardly mobile stand-up comic and roof-runner Toby Foster, another Barnsley lad.

His feeling on achievement in his life so far is that he is living the dream, and being paid to do what he does is more like a bonus. My feeling is that he has a lot further to go. Even in this enlightened age of broadcasting his refusal to upgrade his accent could have been problematical were it not tempered by his other abilities. For now he is keen to go on increasing listening figures, identifying guests and new talents to make a range of contributions to an equally wide range of programmes. Introducing a continuous flow of new young listeners without losing the long-standing more mature audience is not an easy task. His adroitness in providing nostalgic pleasure whilst introducing a new generation to the joys of *Hancock's Half-Hour, Round the Horn, The Goon Show* and the rest is re-assuring. His style is his own and completely unlike that of another Barnsley broadcaster, Jenni Murray. He is essentially a Barnsley man and I believe always will be, wherever chance and talent continue to take him.

4
Jenni Murray

Journalist and BBC presenter

The Japanese do it, the French do it, people from Barnsley do it too. They have two forms of language, which Bernstein called restricted and elaborated speech. It is the difference between the familial, familiar or informal way we sometimes speak, as opposed to the more formal, educated mode of speech or register. So it is with broad Yorkshire and Standard English.

Locally, the elaborated form of speech is taught neither early nor widely enough, in my view. For some it then becomes an obstacle they choose not to overcome, or lack the confidence or opportunity. This in turn becomes a restriction in terms of maximising their potential, possibly in Barnsley, but without doubt outside the town. I would hate to see our old dialect, or any other, at risk of disappearing altogether, but I do believe the acquisition of what amounts to a second language, Standard English, should be a taught core skill for all. David Markwell loves the dialect, but speaks the other when needed. So many of the people to whom I have spoken report early difficulties in making themselves understood, or feeling insecure or inadequate because of it, particularly when they move away to further their education or career.

Jenni Bailey had a mother who was aware of this, and understood the difficulties her daughter could encounter in achieving her dream. The girl sat with an ear glued to the wireless for hours, listening intently to the dulcet tones of Jean Metcalfe and Margery Anderson. She knew then that she didn't want to do anything else, but sound like them, and do what they did. Unusually, she also recognised from an early age that she sounded nothing like them, but would have to learn to. It was, therefore, no problem to her when her mother suggested elocution lessons with Miss Firth, Speech and Drama Coach, just up the hill in Birdwell.

Vowel-sounding practice for her, was as pleasurable and rewarding as hours of kicking a ball at a garage door would have been to the young David Beckham. Ragged rascals running after Rosa in her dress of mauve, going rather fast in Pa's car, really meant something. Like a prodigy with piano scales she practised with a purpose. There were traps to avoid, new sound combinations and emphases to learn. One by one she mastered them, and loved it. Random samples of short or long vowels held less terror for her in time, though Jenni Murray, as she is best known is still wary of them to this day.

School girl Jenni Murray front row first left, with Maureen Wood back row third from left. *Maureen Wood's collection*

Girls at primary school at the same time remember her voice even at that early age. One who admired it then and still does today was Maureen Morris, now Maureen Wood, a tireless voluntary community worker and teacher who had no aspiration to change her own voice, but did have an equally strong and early love of language. For her the dream was to become a teacher, and to share her love of literature, and in particular, Shakespeare. From that early awareness, she missed no opportunity to hear Shakespeare spoken and see it performed well, which finally led to her own moment in the Hall of Fame. Virtually single-handedly in 2000, she not only ran a successful campaign to bring The Royal Shakespeare Company to Barnsley, but offered to put up her entire savings including her recently won alimony, as collateral to achieve it. The week of performances at Darton High School, where she was a Governor, sold out instantly, it was the hottest ticket in town. Every performance was packed with local school parties and enthusiastic, thirsting audiences belying the myth that Barnsley does not want, or deserve, top class theatre of its own. Maureen Wood makes several trips a year herself to Stratford with family and friends, to enjoy the RCS's productions, but feels passionately on behalf of those who cannot do that, and as she puts it, are entitled to.

Jenni Bailey, was equally confident that her entitlement was met, as her love of drama and language spoken equisitely, was founded in those early days. It was Miss Firth's practice to take her pupils to Sheffield to see a range of memorable productions at the city's theatres. Outstanding still in Jenni Murray's mind is seeing Othello brought to life by Laurence Olivier. There was no way back after that.

Secondary school was relatively mundane, she recalls, not just for her, but for all the girls. The arrival of a new French mistress, who was actually French, changed her mind. 'She wore Givenchy perfume, looked like Juliette Greco, told us to put our text books away, and from that minute nothing but French was spoken again'. It was not just style and glamour though, Jeanette Short had a sharp intellect and was a brilliantly challenging motivator. Keen to learn, and now to please, Jenni Murray found confirmation, for her already rooted and still growing certainty, the spoken word was to be important in her life. She was perhaps given a different, but equally clear direction by another teacher whose comment on a written assignment was nothing if not prophetic. It referred to her writing interesting stories, but being somewhat cavalier with the facts; and suggested that she might consider journalism as a career. She did.

First though, she needed more than aspiration, enthusiasm and talent. She needed formal qualification. Her choice of university was not in the South of England, but some eighty miles or so to the east in Hull, on what was still the coast of Yorkshire. Her chosen, specialisms of French and Drama were unsurprising when you consider the credit she gives to Madame Short and Miss Firth. By 1972 with a degree in French she was ready for the BBC but they were not yet ready for her. She rationalises now, she lacked certain pre-requisites of the day for entrée, like the Oxbridge Factor, oral silver cutlery and genuine plumminess. Worst of all she was not and never could be 'one of the boys'. Newsreading by a woman was not to come to the BBC until a year later.

BBC Radio Bristol had no such reservations, so it was there she began a career in radio, learning her craft well, until she moved to television in 1985. The BBC's *South Today* widened her experience, but she found it less comfortable than radio. It was, for her, less her style, even intrusive, in that it tended to dwell on the presenter rather than the subject matter. Within two years she returned to radio as co-presenter, with John Humphrys, to the popular and prestigious Saturday edition of *Today*. The contrasting styles were a successful combination, and all the previous effort, learning, and groundwork she had put in paid off. She was where she had always wanted to be, and where she knew she would be able to produce her best results.

Her presenting style, of serious challenge without the distraction of confrontation, was, and remains valued as highly by listeners as by controllers. She was an absolute natural for *Woman's Hour*, projecting ideal personification of its target audience. Unflappable, caring, probing, informed, attentive and delivering the goods, with a mellifluous voice that sounds as if it is as solid as Blackpool Tower, and is stamped through like a stick of rock, with integrity. Her recollection is that she had a strong female perspective but missed out all that female eunuch stuff. Just as her early experience had taught her she didn't have to choose between being a blonde bimbo or a bloke, she set her own course in a time of sea change. Equal pay, equal opportunities, were on the way in, sex discrimination on the way out. Societal changes were reflected in productions and women's less strident voices became more clearly heard.

Her own contributions are wide ranging in both content, and style, nicely pointed, and frequently, sharply humorous. She has become the experienced, totally dependable voice of women through publications as diverse as *A History of Women Since World War Two* and her publication, *Is it Hot in Here? A Modern Guide to the Menopause*. She is columnist for several newspapers and Eve magazine. Her perspectives are valued, her opinions sought, and her output is prolific.

Though not one to suffer fools gladly, she gives her time readily to causes she believes in, and is Vice President of the Family Planning Association and the Parkinson's Disease Society. Her relaxation is done through needlepoint, knitting and her great love of horses. Her passion for the theatre remains as strong as ever it was.

An honary doctorate from the University of Bradford, is recognition of her work, and her ability to reach a wide audience is reflected in her award of a D. Univ. from The Open University. She is quick to spot what has true staying power, and what is a flash in the pan. Her very early meeting with the women, now internationally admired and lionised with the release of the film of their story *Calendar Girls*, brought spontaneous approval and mutual respect. Jenni Murray found Trish Stewart's idea witty, and Terry Logan's photographic work in the calendar utterly beautiful, describing it as the repossession of the middle aged female form.

She considers herself fortunate to have followed groundbreakers like Sheila Treacey who broke the mould by being the first woman newsreader. Her admiration, interestingly, embraces fellow presenter Sue McGregor, and I see similarities, both are extremely attractive women who chose to work in a medium where their appearance counted for nothing. Both are also able to mask the undercurrents of passionate, personal feelings and views behind the panacea of professionalism. Sue McGregor readily lent her support to help raising girls' expectations in Grimethorpe after the closure of the pits, and Jenni Murray remains a ready and reliable source of expatriot support for the town.

She returned for the final Old Girls' Reunion of her school in 2001, where she spoke engagingly about her memories of the place and people, and stirringly about her hopes for the future generations of girls from the town. When I ask how they can achieve she advises, 'Despite everything, I always just knew that the Beatles had not really broken down the barriers for us all. Luckily my Mother suspected it far sooner and prepared me for what we both knew I would always do. That was a great start, but there's been a great deal of hard work and more than one glass ceiling on the way'. No surprises there.

What really did surprise me though, was that this woman with a broadcasting reputation second to none, and a voice to die for, worries about how she sounds, and still edits out phrases like cut foot and misses every bus after years of perfect diction. It was no surprise to find the BBC website of famous radio presenters had just two whose listing begins by declaring that they were born in Barnsley. The one that most people would never have guessed after hearing her speak is Jenni Murray OBE.

Jenni Murray addresses the final old girls' reunion at Barnsley Girls High School, watched by Kathryn Badrack one of the organisers, and a former Miss Yorkshire Television finalist.
Maureen Wood

5
Jane Sanderson

Producer BBC Radio

In the next village to where Jenni Murray had her first elocution lessons, a generation later, was another girl who also decided that journalism was to be her future.

Her mother, Anne Wildsmith, had left school at sixteen and taken a job with the National Coal Board. It seemed by the school's yardstick that she had done well. By the time she was thirty, married to Bob Sanderson, and bringing up two daughters, Jane and Jackie, she knew she had under achieved. She went back into education with a vengeance, training to become a teacher. Rapid success and advancement took her to a Headship, a Senior Lectureship at Sheffield Hallam University and then posts as an English Advisor and subsequently Inspector with the Local Education Authority. An acknowledged authority on language development, Anne Sanderson's work on reading and writing skills is

Eileen Ellis and Ann Sanderson have been involved in working with local children voluntarily and professionally for most of their lives. *Mike Swallow*

internationally acclaimed and she has made inputs to Educational Training half way round the world and back.

It was inevitable living in such a family that the girls would be surrounded by books, literacy, reading, writing delivered daily like the milk. Equally predictable was that writing might become the preferred career option for at least one of them. When Jane Sanderson completed her career profile at school, it was returned to her as incomplete, because she had entered only one choice, journalism. The explanation was simple for her, but a problem for them, she had entered the only career in which she was interested, or intended to follow.

'Journalism is a hobby, not a career. Think of something else', came the considered response. This surely could not be Kenny Doughty's career advisor. With the same logic as a young Albert Ramsbottom exploring the somnambulant posture of Wallace the lion, it just didn't seem right to the child. Not wishing to appear argumentative, but assertive enough not to accept defeat at the first hurdle, her response was utter logic. 'We get *The Guardian* every day, and somebody must be writing it'.

Her starting point was a degree in English at the University of Leicester, and with a mind as focussed as her purpose she applied to the BBC for a place on their Graduate Training Programme. She felt it would be the ideal training for her avowed intention of working for the company at some point in her career. She was delighted to be asked to attend for interview, and optimistic, enthusiastic and ready to start, she arrived in London. Looking back, she describes it as one of the most awful experiences of her life. Her degree had qualified her well in English, but journalistically she felt totally out of her depth. She knew the interview was going badly, but could not retrieve it. Humbled, with self confidence at rock bottom, not accepted for the programme, she was now at a turning point. Should she persist or accept that she was not cut out for the business?

It is at such times that real tenacity comes into play. Her recollection is that though the experience was excruciatingly painful, it was not without its benefits. Still totally set on the career, she set about putting right what might have been the problem. She felt she was not well enough prepared for the specialism required in the interview, and sought the advice of a journalist, the father of one of her friends. His line was direct and encouraging, she should not give up hope, but show her persistence. She should learn the trade by working in it, learning everything she could about it, and then return to the BBC if that was still what she wanted to do. She would then have the skills, experience and renewed confidence to show what she already believed and he did, that she was made of the right stuff.

She laughs at the unspectacular start she made with her first publication, the *Hardware Trade Journal*. 'It was not what I had been dreaming about since I was small. It was a bit like one of those journals

Role models in action Sgt. Keith Ellis B.E.M and Dorothy Hyman, Olympic Medallist. *The author*

you see on *Have I Got News For You*, but actually it was a very good start in the business. Six of us began together and were put on a very structured and formal training programme. It covered everything we would need to know from short-hand to publishing law. It was also good fun, we were like minded as a group and all got on really well. It was a happy introduction, but it wasn't where I could stay for the rest of my life'.

She was actually sorry to leave the team but when an opportunity arose to join the *Oxford Star and Mail* she went for it. This was a different kind of reporting and investigating, and a new learning curve, of deadlines and headlines, creating news, or finding it like a sniffer dog. She recalls a squirmingly bad experience of being sent out on a story that she did not want to cover, but had to. Someone had spotted an advertisement in the sales section of the newspaper, 'Wedding dress size 12 for sale. Unworn'. She really did not want to know the answer to the question she was required to pose, why was it not worn? Adding this to the fact that she felt that her feet were paddling like mad to keep her head above water, she moved again.

The *Hampstead and Highgate Express* offered a wider range of experience, combining routine local issues with welcome opportunities to interview people like Fay Weldon, Melvyn Bragg, Michael Foot, for a completely different, very aware and influential readership. It provided an excellent grounding for her next career move, which led her finally to where she had always said she would be, with the BBC. Already established as a journalist, the next six months were shared between experience in radio, and television on the *Breakfast Programme*. She preferred radio, finding more writing and editing involved there than in TV. What she had developed from that first defeat at the BBC was to play to her strengths, rather than to opt for her preferences. The tenacity and persistence had paid off, and she was delighted to join *The World at One*, as a junior producer.

Working alongside the big boys, she found pressure on a new scale. High powered, highly competitive and macho, it was an invaluable start to her broadcasting career. To start off by working with James Naughtie was both rewarding and exciting for a young producer. Challenged by the pace and also the quality of the programme, she feels now it was of enormous benefit to her in terms of character building, but also as a professional experience. In time the diet of politics and current affairs, together with finding bright, different ways of presenting the same stories, or similar ones, held less charm for her, and she readily accepted an offer to produce 'Woman's Hour.'

The programme's eclectic mix was refreshing, more interesting, if equally demanding. The range of subjects and guests in just one programme could be as diverse as snowdrops, cabinet ministers, philately and Caesarean sections, but she felt at once that the format, style and challenge there were better matched to her own strengths and preferences. Despite shared roots and a background in news and current affairs she was apprehensive of starting work with high-powered and very successful Jenni Murray. She rates her as one of three all-time great female voices of radio, the others being Murray's own former heroines, Sue McGregor and Jean Metcalfe. 'Her inflection is unique, she places emphasis in different points of sentences, that no one else would think of, and she does it without thinking. I used to try to sound like her, but it was hopeless so I quickly gave up on that'.

The time and place was right for Sanderson's own early set goal to be reached. She loved the challenges, the team and the results. It entailed chasing people and stories, putting the right voice with the right sound effects and ensuring the questions posed brought out the best response without imposing slant. Pre-recorded interviews allowed the luxury of editing out ums and ers, saving precious seconds, but also streamlining what was broadcast. The producer's role, less apparent to the listener, is wider than I had imagined until I heard her enthuse about its totality and how satisfying the technicalities behind a successful radio production are. It becomes clear that two of the BBC's most respected radio productions owe their success, in part, to two very determined women from Barnsley.

6
Philip Mosley

Artistic Co-ordinator, The Royal Ballet

Even outside, the Royal Opera House has a magical feel. Inside, newly restored, magnificent, opulent, a spectacle worth seeing, even without a performance. It is not just the beauty of the place, or even the thought of who has performed or visited; from the minute you walk through the stage door you can see the affection, hear the pride, feel the partnership. Everyone wants you to love the place as much as they do. It's frantic but welcoming, and you feel a part of the place instantly. As Philip Mosley joins us, a complete stranger shows a book on the table beside us, clearly beside herself with delight. He makes her day complete by complimenting her on being mentioned in it, before beginning our tour of The House.

The place is vast and bustling, although there is no performance that night. It's not unlike an old mining village, everyone we pass speaks, and some, overhearing the guided tour, add their own special comment or favourite story. It is ridiculous to believe you are a part of it, but you feel you really are. The ultimate fantasy though, is when we suddenly find ourselves standing centre stage with the house lights full on. It is breath taking, and plays havoc with the imagination. I, who have never had a dancing lesson in my life, and now have a useless leg, and a bus pass, momentarily believe the impossible. With one flying leap I could be into an effortless *pas de deux* with him and bring the full house to its feet before swanning off with an armful of flowers to

Philip Mosley on the stage of The Royal Opera House, Covent Garden where he has regularly danced for over twenty five years, with the magnificent performer's view of the auditorium behind him. *The author*

waiting chilled champagne and adoring fans. The moment passes, reason prevails and self-indulgence is limited to a photograph taken with him, to impress my grandchildren. I then take the picture I am really there for, to illustrate the story of the real Billy Elliott.

It is a long and winding road from Barnsley to where he now stands, but he made it. He was two and a half years old and had never seen live dancing, but was fascinated by TV. Just like my grandson, Benny, he watched films with Gene Kelly or Donald O'Connor, Dick Van Dyke or Fred Astaire, from the age of two and tried to dance like them, he wanted to be a song and dance man, not a ballet dancer. Then, he stood and watched his sister Anita's dancing class and was totally hooked. By the time he was three he had begun, not ballet but tap and modern classes, whilst his twin brother Paul showed no interest at all. Another Barnsley winner did though, Jonathan Ellis sang and danced through a variety of stage and TV successes to where he is today, supporting Kevin Kline's first tap dancing role in the new film of Cole Porter's life story.

Philip Mosley's dancing teacher was Ros Wicks, who had an eye for talent and a gift for bringing it out in her young charges. Slowly he was persuaded to try ballet and proved very able, but still loved the rhythm, the noise, the vibration, the beat and the swinging movement of modern and tap dancing.

Jonathan Ellis visits Bretton Hall as a positive role model to motivate youngsters from the area, watched by Olympic medallist Dorothy Hyman and local company directors Barry and Aileen Cook, who also took part. Children were captivated by his description of the exhilaration of success after playing in *Pyjama Game* and *Blood Brothers* in the West End and on tour. *The author*

He had no idea at that stage that he was talented. He recalls school concerts where he felt he was 'wheeled out' to do his speciality numbers, but says he always refused to do ballet. He is clear, it was not because he feared ridicule, but he knew, even then, what he was best at and at that point in his life, it was not ballet. By the time he was ten, it was and at a Dance Festival in Leeds, another child's parent approached Margaret and Albert Mosley to suggest he audition for the Royal Ballet School. Immediately supportive and keen to encourage their child's talent, they applied, he auditioned and was accepted.

For his parents though it was an awful dilemma. They were proud and delighted by his success, united in unqualified support, but equally apprehensive about letting him go so far away on his own. Reminding him constantly that he was only a phone call away, and that his father would be there in three hours if he wanted to come home, was the only way they could all handle the wrench of the move to White Lodge and the new life. He, who had never experienced ridicule for his dancing, now had to learn to cope with mockery of his Barnsley accent. Nobody could understand me, he tells me in soft standardised diction, 'I had to say everything at least twice. They were mostly from middle class areas and without strong regional accents, they just couldn't handle my dialect'. He was nick named Geeore or Tuthingy, he recalls, but with no show of lasting pain or damage. 'It actually helped, it toughened me up, it's what kids are like whether they're in Barnsley or at The Royal School of Ballet'.

There were edges to be rubbed off the raw youngster, he remembers, laughing at himself, and his lack of knowledge in his first lessons at the Royal Ballet School. He heard the story of Swan Lake for the first time with total disbelief, certain that no kid at his previous school would have accepted a word of it. Putting his previous life on hold, he undertook the tough and gruelling regime of ballet training, and loved it.

Increasingly successful, he was eventually chosen for a month's exchange visit to China, followed a year later by what remains his longest tour abroad. The Americas; New York, Boston, Cleveland, Clearwater, Sarasota, Miami, Mexico City and Caracas were brilliant, but for him the spectacle of arriving in Rio de Janeiro with dawn breaking over the Statue of Christ the Redeemer remains unforgettable. Australia and every other continent followed as he danced, literally, around the world. He dances less now, but in his mid-thirties would anticipate that.

A dream come true is his recent appointment as Artistic Co-ordinator for the Royal Ballet. Having spent most of his life there he is unable to visualise himself anywhere else, and calls it his home. His ties with Barnsley remain strong, especially since the recent death of his father. Speaking at the funeral he gratefully reminded the world that no other parent in their village would have done what his father and mother had done for him. In unhesitatingly supporting his son's unusual skill and his new life without objection, Albert Mosley had instinctively given him the confidence and courage to achieve everything he has achieved.

He is unspoilt, and completely unaffected in telling me of dancing for The Queen, Princess Margaret, The Queen Mother, Princess Diana, Ex President and Mrs Clinton at the White House and celebrities too numerous to mention. His proudest moments are still when he knows his mother is in the audience at the Royal Opera House, knowing exactly how she will feel. She tells me how excited she gets waiting for the curtain to rise, wanting to tell everyone that he is her son, and 'if they are chatty and friendly I do!' He will dance again on that stage this winter, still thrilled as much as thrilling.

Philip Mosley whose career took off with a dramatic leap. *Simon Rae-Scott*

Invited by Darcy Bussell to accompany her to the premier of *Billy Elliott*, he saw few real parallels with his own life, but thought that unimportant. What is of real importance he believes, is in the past two years the number of boys from similar backgrounds taking up ballet has leapt dramatically, just like he does.

7
Mick McCarthy

Football Manager

As I struggle with the decision of whether to have my salad sandwich with or without mayonnaise, Gaynor Sawyer at Designer Sandwich has no doubts at all. 'Mick McCarthy, best player Barnsley's had in my lifetime'. She has had longer to decide though, ever since she had the photo which has stood next to the fish tank on her mother's sideboard for twenty years, taken with the player who is still her footballing hero. 'He was hard but fair, totally dependable and popular, but never big headed,' she recalls, adding 'he was the best looking as well, all the girls liked him but he never seemed to notice.' That was of course because he has been in love with Fiona, his wife, since they were in the same class at primary school.

Arthur Bower's decision is, possibly, based on more objective indicators. A life-long Reds' fan, Bower's collection of information, memorabilia and observations are filed as accessibly in his head as in his impressive filing system. He is the club's unofficial historian having

Michael Parkinson and Arthur Bower, still in touch. *Arthur Bower*

collaborated on several interviews, books and publication about the club's legends. George and Ted Robledo, Tommy Taylor, now ranked as one of the best three forwards ever to play for Manchester United, and the magical Johnny Kelly and others immortalised by and immortalising Michael Parkinson.

Without hesitation, Bower says 'A two hundred per cent man, Mick McCarthy, I have never seen anybody give as much as him, he gives his all every single game, always has done. I have always had the view that he would manage Barnsley one day, I wish he would. 'He was the man of bronze for me, the Jim Thorpe of football.' It is a widely held view in the town, it is impossible to overstate the esteem in which McCarthy is held. He is remembered as one who has never changed, honest, uncompromising but never dirty, shrewd and totally committed.

Steadfastly declining to consider his life in celebrity terms, and strengthened by his working class roots, which are not humble, he rejects a life style that would undermine his inbred family values. He has simply had, and taken, the opportunity to work his way up his chosen ladder, and enjoys his local, league and international sporting record. The trappings that come with it, like loss of privacy, time away from home, and media intrusion, are less enjoyable, but a fact of life. His view is you are there to look as if you're going to win, and do it.

He looks back to his first captaincy and grins. Selected by new headteacher, Mary Kitching at Our Lady's Junior School football team, he says he knew then it was for him. He is generous in his identification of people who inspired, motivated or just believed in him. She was the first he recalls, and he never forgot it, and to her delight thanked her every time she watched him play, even when he became captain of first division Barnsley.

Others followed, like Les Foweather under whose guidance Worsborough High School 'won everything' in the Yorkshire schoolboys' league, and sharpened McCarthy's appetite for success. Not yet fantastic, but Captain Promising without a doubt, and additionally coached by Maurice Taylor he tried for Barnsley Boys. Exhilarated by the prospect of success, he was equally devastated aged sixteen to be let go from the final short list of twenty. Recalling the experience he expresses reservations about today's system of identification of potential in players as young as seven or eight. Building dreams and aspirations on too wide a base, without proper consideration of the impact of inevitable 'failure' for a percentage of children troubles him. The nets are so huge, he feels, it is easier to win through to temporary success, but hates the thought of any child feeling as he did when turned down for Barnsley Boys. There is a fine balance against this and early identification and input for the Beckhams of this world. He sees too the necessity of the right temperament for the game, or at least the ability to grow with it. A goalie can have thirty clean sheets, but with one bad miss he might as well be dead and has to be able to live with it. What is often forgotten in the game these days, he feels, is that effectiveness is more important than just looking good.

He has learned this because he did not give up on football despite the early rejection. Playing for local club teams he met Keith Steele, who seeing his potential, encouraged, coached and advised him. At sixteen he had to make the big decision. £35 a week and a respected qualification at the end of an apprenticeship with the NCB, or £14 a week as an apprentice footballer with Barnsley. He didn't need Steele's backing but he had it, and went to Oakwell. He reckons it was Steele's faith in him that enabled him to ignore the teacher who told him he would never make a footballer. There he met Norman Rimmington, who he credits as the biggest single help in his career, and typically has kept in regular contact with throughout the years. 'He was the first person to really make me feel I could play,' he says of his years with the ex-goalie, then head groundsman, and now friend.

The rest is a matter of local history from that first game against Chesterfield at home, with the first goal scored by McCarthy. If there had ever been a moment of doubt, he now passed the point of no return. Progress and maturation led him to first team squad to club captain, still learning all the way from Barry Murphy and Eric Winstanley, and with memories of former Barnsley heroes Danny Blanchflower and Norman Smith.

Alan Clarke's spell as manager at Oakwell opened his eyes to a more modern and professional style of leadership, improving facilities, presentation and status, and was continued by Clarke's former Leeds team mate Norman Hunter when he in turn took over the Reds with coach Ian Evans. Evans became a long-term friend and is now McCarthy's trusted colleague and assistant manager. Following a suspension, McCarthy was unable to get straight back into the first team due to his replacement's sound performance within the team. He had also become a desirable signing and Manchester City beat Newcastle adding him to their squad, followed by Celtic and Millwall. The turning point in his life though came when he was picked for the squad for the Republic of Ireland by Jack Charlton.

Solid performances paid off and he became part of the Republic of Ireland's team in the European Championships. Success there not only allowed him to sample the frenzied adulation of success at that level, but led to the ultimate dream, being one of the few to captain a national team to the final of the World Cup. The euphoria of that moment lives on in his mind, including the salt taste of defeat. They did their best and were one unbelievable step from being the best team in the world, with a Barnsley-born captain, and a manager, Jack Charlton, who chose to live in the town for years.

Conveniently on the road to Sheffield is a good fishing ground that has spawned some of the world's finest coarse fishermen. Founder of the legendary Barnsley Blacks, Dick Clegg has been twice honoured for his contribution to the sport as England's team manager with an MBE and an OBE. Other names like Dennis White, England team member Tom Pickering, former World Champion, and Alan Scotthorne the only man to be World Champion three years in succession, all part of the Barnsley Team's fame. These are names that send ripples of admiration across the fishing world earning respect equal to that of either Charlton brother in footballing folk law. Their combined efforts have won more individual and team gold awards than any other sporting team in UK history. Not many got away from them.

Charlton's success with the Irish team put him into a category of adulation normally reserved for The Pope, St Patrick, Parnell, and slightly higher than the nation's great writers Wilde, Shaw, Joyce, Yeats. It ranks as one of the most unbelievable moments in his life, the day the lad from Our Lady's Infants was presented to The Pope.

Replacing Charlton on his retirement, McCarthy's performance as manager was statistically better than his. A month before the 2002 World Cup he was hailed for masterminding the Republic's outstanding performance 19 wins out of 20 games. Being a big enough man to put the team before any consideration of his own, he was generous in his public praise of Roy Keane.

His experience tells him being a good manager is as much about providing the right position, the motivation and the team spirit as anything. Play Rivaldo at left back and you would not have the best player in the world in 2002. He speaks of George Best with a different singular kind of admiration because on the field, Best was the most reliable genius of his day, possibly of anybody's day. He did not play remarkably well one day and then disappoint the next, but was totally consistent. He never failed to deliver, to amaze, to confound. He was the stuff that dreams are made of, not just passing coruscation. And significantly he notes, a great team player in a team game can make other players look almost as good as he is, knowing when to take but also the moment to pass to someone else. For such men Mick McCarthy reserves his highest praise, the players who give their all and deliver week in week out. For him consistency is as important as talent, and I'm reminded of Arthur Bower's view of him.

Superstardom is different now he believes. He won't go down that road he calls Hovis mentality, of borrowed kits and missing studs, those days are well gone. He does however recall playing in an international match when the team was asked to donate their fees to charity. One young Irish player pale-faced and panic stricken, hastily rang his wife to establish whether she had paid cash or credit card for their new fridge. Players at that time had financial worries of a different order to deal with, not enough money, rather than too much.

He is philosophical about life and the game now, wiser, experienced and phlegmatic. As we talk, a call on his mobile tells him, Howard

Mick McCarthy with local pal Glyn Robinson, on one of their regular visits to Barnsley's Living Well. *The author*

Wilkinson has been given the Sunderland job, neither of us suspecting for a minute, that he will have that very job in a matter months. This is a killing game as well as the best in the world, eighteen wins on the trot for Ireland, the law of averages tells him it must be nearly his turn to be got at. Regret doesn't make you a better footballer, but his only regret is that by his score, he wasn't 'the best'.

Not everyone agrees with him. Irish by birth, Barnsley by adoption, one fanatical football fan by instinct, is adamant. Charlton was the archetypal hero who was given every accolade for what he did for the Irish team. He left an established, improved but ageing stable as his legacy. Mick McCarthy, however, he regards as having constructed a new foundation that carries his own brand and impetus, reforming the team with the young blood that is there to be built on by Brian Kerr.

Half Barnsley, half Irish, a combination that delights and suits McCarthy. The Irish half loves the craic, making music and living life to the full. His speech though is not the gentle Irish brogue, it is the less loved Barnsley accent. I ask him if it is the thing he would like to have changed. He is adamant in his refuting of the idea. 'Barnsley, whatever else it is known for, is famous for straight talking and honesty, it's a definite advantage in this business, I'm Irish in Ireland, but I don't do the Blarney'. It was not Blarney he met or responded with in the World Cup in 2002, it was Barnsley bottle that decided enough was enough and sent home a recalcitrant megastar. I tell him he is now widely considered one of Barnsley's best, but he defends by naming others he thinks more deserving. I swerve and wing the pass of evidenced research, but he blocks and scores in the closing seconds of the game, using the Blarney he disclaims. 'I learned a long time ago never to argue with a woman, and especially I wouldn't try it with one from Barnsley.' Gaynor was right.

8
Dickie Bird

Cricket Umpire and Author

He was named Harold Dennis, Harold after his father and his Mother's favourite name, Dennis, but everyone including The Queen, has always called him 'Dickie' Bird. It started when he went to Burton Road Junior and Infant School, where they had no pitch on which to play either cricket or football. It followed him to Raley Secondary Modern where they played both sports, but on the same pitch because there was only one. He found he liked both sports equally, and was equally good at both. Playing for hours between two sets of jumpers, or at a wicket chalked on a wall, brought their rewards. He signed for Barnsley FC aged fifteen, in preference to a choice of six first division clubs. His life was to be Barnsley Cricket Club in summer, and football in winter. Only six months later an injury to his cartilage ruled football out, leaving him to make a good enough recovery to continue playing cricket.

Years later he rationalises, 'You had to fight for everything just to survive in those days. Life was tough for us all, but it made us tough as well. I'd been brought up by my dad, never to give in, so I didn't. I found I had the same kind of grit and determination he had from working underground from the age of thirteen to sixty five. He hated working down the pit, but he did it to earn enough for me to be kitted up for cricket. Families like ours didn't have a spare set of pads or whites in the wardrobe, and it was serious money to provide a start for me in the game. I have never forgotten what sacrifices my whole family made for me, that meant I had to make a success of it, so they hadn't done it all for nothing. I did what I had to do to get my leg sorted out, so I could go on with cricket, though my footballing was finished'.

The memory of his first attempt to get into the exclusive world of League Cricket still pains him. Inspired by Len Hutton he presented himself at Shaw Lane for a trial for the Yorkshire League. 'I just knew that I had the ability to play at that level,' he remembers, 'but that day taught me that ability is nothing in sport, life or work, without mental strength, the urge to win and some one to believe in you'. His attempt was dismissed, and he was turned away more miserable than he had ever been in his life. He would have walked away from cricket that day, but bumped into local cricketer, Alf Broadhead, on his way out of the ground. Broadhead asked him what the problem was, and on hearing of his experience, insisted on taking him back. He then spent hours in the nets

As he is best known Dickie Bird. *Dickie Bird's collection*

bowling to him, encouraging him and finally motivating him back into the game.

Bird showed great promise as the first nineteen year old to open for Yorkshire, but in reality would have been just another professional cricketer. That is not how he became a name that is recognised world wide, wherever the game is played. Despite playing innumerable matches for his County before moving to Leicestershire his name would have been remembered mostly by fellow Yorkshiremen, but have been relatively unremarkable. It was the move to umpiring that changed his world and his life forever. That came about because John Warr, fast bowler Middlesex and England, suggested it. Originally laughing it off, second thoughts changed his mind. In August 1969 he applied to Lords for consideration for the First Class County Umpires List. He was accepted immediately, within eighteen months had achieved Test Match Status, and the rest is history.

I ask him if, off the pitch, he is a compulsive worrier. 'Worrier? I can witter for England. If I haven't anything to worry about, I invent something,' he admits, implicitly accepting ridicule it may invite. Only those of us who have to be at a railway station an hour before the train is due can be expected to understand this. In his case it is best illustrated by the first of many visits to Buckingham Palace. The invitation was to a private luncheon with The Queen and Prince Edward. He left the house at 5 a.m. to take the train from Wakefield, arrived at King's Cross at 8.20 a.m, took a taxi, and was standing outside the Palace gates at 8.40 a.m. promptly.

There he explained the purpose of his visit to the policeman on duty, whose official response was 'You're a bit early Dickie, we haven't changed the Guard yet and we can't stop that'. Left, with only one option, he took up a deep field position in a coffee shop across Buckingham Palace Road. There he sat for the next four hours, drinking cups of coffee, before making a return run across the road, this time to be given access to the Palace. 'Well you'd better have a drink,' said the Queen sipping a glass of Campari and soda, as the relieved guest finally arrived and recounted his journey. 'The punctuality thing became an issue when I started umpiring. It would have been unthinkable to turn up late, so I always got there earlier than I had to. It's become nearly an obsession now though'.

If you ask him how to become a successful umpire, he will tell you instantly that the first thing you have to do is to forget that you ever played the game yourself. There are characteristics that he regards as crucial, and high on his list are consistency and fairness, but he also includes honesty, straightforwardness being an essential in Barnsley. Decisions taken with integrity and delivered with politeness, and occasionally humour, are evidence of a sound and strong professional, and also gain the respect of both players and spectators. The worrier is left in the dressing room, it is a very different person who has stepped out into the relentless limelight of some of the world's greatest cricket fixtures. 'Once I walked out onto that pitch I became a different man. The world was mine, it didn't matter what ground or whoever was playing,'. You feel instinctively that he prefers being that man.

To any impartial observer his list of record achievements is both spectacular and unique. He is the only man in the world to have umpired three world cup finals, all at the revered Lords ground, where he is an honorary life member of the MCC. He is also an honorary life member of both Yorkshire and Leicestershire Cricket Clubs and is the only person to have umpired both men's and women's World Cup Finals. He holds the world record, of 68 Test Matches, 92 one-day internationals and 158 international matches. He stood at the Bi-Centenary Test Match between England and The Rest of The World, The Centenary Test March between England and Australia and The Queen's Silver Jubilee Test Match England v Australia in 1977.

From then on few regional or national honours, or awards, have passed him by, including Yorkshire Man of the Year, Yorkshire Personality of the

Dickie Bird receives an Honorary Doctorate from the University of Hallam Sheffield. *Dickie Bird's collection*

Dickie Bird after receiving his M.B.E at Buckingham Palace. *Dickie Bird's collection*

Year, and People of the Year. He has honorary doctorates from the Universities of Leeds and Sheffield Hallam, and is an honorary life member of Cambridge University Cricket Club. His 1997 autobiography is the best-selling sports biography in history, he tells me with pride, that is all the more remarkable considering it was his fourth, following *Not Out, That's out* and *From the Pavilion End*. *White Cap and Bails* completed the fistful in 1999 making him as big a success financially as he was professionally. The latest, *Dickie Bird's Britain*, lists his favourite everythings.

He opened his score of the twenty first century well, with the Barnsley Millennium Award of Merit for outstanding service to the community, and in particular his promotion of civic pride and the image of the borough. It was closely followed by what he regards as one of the greatest moments in a great life. He was made a Freeman of the Borough of Barnsley, the town he has chosen to remain in all his life. You only have to speak his name in India to find he is rated a close second to the cow or the peepul tree in terms of deification. No amount of worship could persuade him to move there permanently, or anywhere else for that matter. His local honours are his greatest source of satisfaction and pride, but he would be a fool not to value the national and international accolades, which he is not. It is also with an equal sense of disbelief that he shows the awards and honours he has been given. He does not mention the additional baggage he is required to carry, that of knowing resentment comes in direct proportion to recognition.

During the last quarter of a century he has been interviewed by every major presenter on national TV and radio, since first being on *Down Your Way* with Brian Johnson in 1975. His list includes Sir David Frost on both *Through the Keyhole* and *Breakfast with Frost*, *Richard and Judy*, Clive Anderson, Clive James and Terry Wogan. A devout Methodist, he bought his house featured with him in *Songs of Praise* not only because it is in Barnsley, but also because Wesley had preached there. He was interviewed by Sue Lawley on *Desert Island Discs* and Sue Barker chaired his appearance on *A Question of Sport*. His favourite one remains receiving the red book on *This is Your Life*, but the highlight of his life was being invested with the MBE by the Queen in 1986.

Journalist and columnist Christa Ackroyd, formerly with Yorkshire Television and now the face of BBC's *Look North* and a Sunday Express columnist, has interviewed the regular guest so often she says she feels like his mother. This is serious enough for her to carry an extra pack of tissues when she knows he is on her list for the day. He is notoriously sentimental and makes no apologies for it. 'I can't help it, some people are overwhelmed by occasions, and I'm just one of them. I have a real problem dealing with it. Sentiment is my defence mechanism against the enormity of some of the things that have happened to me. It's highlighted because I'm in the public eye when it happens'.

Perhaps it is more understandable when he goes on to say, 'I've had a life I couldn't have dreamed of. To do it I lived from the age of nineteen to sixty five out of a suitcase, and I was completely obsessed by cricket. The idea of divorcing cricket was frightening and I would have had to do that even, to some degree, to have had a wife and family. Now I have the scrapbooks of that life but I haven't a son of my own to leave them with. I would have loved to have had a son, not only to follow me, but for me to follow him too. I'd have loved to watch my son play cricket, or any other sport, or do anything else he wanted to do. Maybe he would have wanted to be a sportsman like me, maybe not. But he could have had the scrapbooks and perhaps passed them on to his son as well. Then I would have had a future. As it is, my past is my future'. There speaks a man of both profit and honours in his own county as he celebrates fifty years in cricket.

9
Geoffrey Boycott

Cricket and Commentator

Geoffrey Boycott is not a Barnsley man, despite his early and continuing connection with the town. He is a Yorkshireman. From his earliest schooldays, whilst bright enough to have followed an academic route, he knew it was cricket that would be his passion and the basis of his achievement. Everybody should have a dream to follow is his belief. Perhaps the combination of an innate sense of purpose with the discipline and tenacity, which was a natural by-product of his upbringing, naturally made him the man he is today. What he was in his cricketing life, many believe, was one of the very best batsmen in the world.

Still faithful to the part of the country, in which he was born, he is very much a product of a mining community, and remains solidly proud of it. The typical matriarchal society to which he belonged raised a generation of successful offspring. Grammar School scholarships and post-war socialism translated entitlement into real opportunity for these children. They had a new awareness of their potential, if not always the social skills, eloquence and self-confidence to maximise it. Jenny Boycott was one of a legion of working-class mothers who fitted their children out in expensive school uniforms and sent them out to meet a better future than they themselves had known.

His firm belief still is that he missed out on very little coming from a village close to Barnsley, and being brought up in a mining community. Public school rhetoric, polish and advantage aside, he feels his life there was as happy and complete a start as it could have been. As good as any home in the neighbourhood, it guaranteed and gave understanding, discipline, good plain food on the table every day, clean clothes to go out in and love to come home to. Like thousands of other kids in similar Persil and Bisto families, he learned the rules and conventions of that society early. Being respectable mattered, which entailed respect for oneself, for others and for the ethic of work. Since every other family seemed to be in similar circumstances there was no concept of being disadvantaged or missing out in any way. School extended horizons and introduced competition, and it was there that he learned that life itself is a competition, and that winning is better than losing.

In a tone that still declares respect he remembers his first teachers as role models Mr. Andrews and Mr Weavers, who gave support and encouragement, allowing him to settle and meet the demands of the new life of school. He remains grateful that he went then to Hemsworth Grammar School with its policy of all pupils doing all sports. Being required to take part in cross-country runs strengthened his legs, whilst the strong discipline strengthened in his character, the firm foundations already introduced at home. In this he is the antithesis of Billy Casper, Barry Hines' fictional schoolboy. In Barnsley author Hines book A *Kestrel for a Knave* and the subsequent classic *Kes* adaptation, in Ken Loach's film version, Casper represents the almost inevitable and predictable outcome of a less supportive, structured and secure family background. Boycott intuitively felt, and remains convinced, that young people generally benefit from the discipline, industry and co-ordination that sport provides in all areas of their development. He is convinced too that sport should be a high priority in all schools for all children. He cites the requirement to do soccer, athletics, gym and rugby as well as cricket, as having stretched him mentally as well as physically. It also taught him how to lose, as well as how to win.

Having often wondered myself, I take the opportunity to ask Geoffrey Boycott why it was that, to my knowledge, he had never queried being given out. Playing throughout an era of growing challenge and dissent he remained stoically impassive, even in the face of questionable judgement. 'That's God in a white coat out there,' he replies. 'Once that finger is up, you walk. There's no point in arguing anyway, you're not going to get an umpire to change his mind – not once he's given you out.' I see that point but want to go further into his mind at such times, so persist in asking if he was never angry about it. He agrees he was – but with himself for getting out. He could not justify being angry with a bowler for playing well enough to achieve it, nor with an umpire for giving the decision.

His system was to take the walk back to the pavilion, trying to analyse what he had done wrong. He would then ask team-mates what went wrong with his response to a ball from Bedser, or ask Trueman how he thought Statham had managed to bowl him out. His anger, frustration or whatever negative emotion he had, was thus converted into a more positive learning situation, and he constantly used every defeat to add to his formidable batting skill.

David Sugden recalls watching his own boyhood hero, the upper-school Boycott, practising for hour upon hour, when other members of the school side had long since tired or lost interest. With inspiring determination he would persist until he was satisfied that he made some improvement. That degree of tenacity and dedication was commented on also by Ron Blackburn – himself a fanatical sportsman. He recalls, early in their post-school lives, working in an office with the young Boycott. Having only one in six Saturday mornings off, staff would wheel and deal to change or avoid them. Boycott would work anyone else's in order to add to his own holiday allocation the accumulated days off in lieu. He would then use the hard-won time to ensure his availability for selection in Yorkshire Second Eleven two-day matches.

In those early days he is also remembered at Barnsley Golf Club, adding yet another sport to his list. He was remarkable because he played the course alone. A solitary figure for much of the time, he preferred to improve his game to the point of playing well, mastering his defects before he felt ready to compete with others. Then he could relax, share the game, and go on learning from it. I remember exhorting my then very young, but keen, golfing son to watch him and learn how to win, as much as how to play golf, which he did, and at fourteen became the youngest player to win the Club's Members' Trophy. Boycott readily states that he has always found this level of effort to be necessary for him, to offset the fact that he is 'not a natural'. Bearing this view in mind, it is all the more commendable that he had the ability to identify his strengths and apply them to mould himself into a skilful professional of world-class status. Not without cost though. With the universal gift of hindsight, but with no trace of regret, he now acknowledges that he sacrificed much of the social life that other youngsters enjoyed outside the demands of a sporting career.

Trips into Barnsley town centre for him were not to Pallister's Temperance Bar in Regent Street South with hundreds of his contemporaries drinking hot cordials. He was not in the queue for the magnificent Ritz cinema with its amazing chandeliers and mirrored staircases that begged to be danced down Busby Berkley style. He did not applaud and sing along to the mighty Wurlitzer organ as it rose to the strains of *Blaze Away*, played by Trevor Willetts or Ernest Exley. Not for him was the Tuesday night Beginners' Class at the Cuban Ballroom where stumbling quick-steppers and Lingering Blues lurchers practised their skills in preparation for the Friday night live performances under the rotating glitter ball, and the

Ernest Exley who with Trevor Willetts, is remembered for providing musical entertainment during the intervals of performances at the Ritz Cinema. *Marjorie Exley's collection*

watchful eyes of dancing instructors and proprietors, Mavis Burrows and Bill Ball. He would not even be one of the aspiring sophisticates drinking Gin and French or Gin and It and fox-trotting at the more urbane Three Cranes Hotel. The young Geoffrey was much more likely to be found at Shaw Lane Cricket Club in the company of the two Dickies – Bird and Wilkinson, Eddie Ledgard and the rest, practising until the light had gone, and then talking cricket.

To keep that dedication, when all about him were losing theirs, was no real effort to him since he was in love with the game. It was not a sacrifice but a natural, innate inclination with which he was born. He is strongly on the side of nature in the nature versus nurture debate. Whilst accepting the influence and value of sound role modelling as positive elements in his development, he is constant in his belief that we are what we are born with, and born to be. A crucial part of his personal philosophy is that we take those gifts, and use them throughout our lives, to face whatever adversities we have to face individually. The only real difference between people is how they deal with what life presents. In the year of 2003 his philosophy, he told me is that we pick ourselves up and get on with living; there is dramatic irony for you!

Of the twelve Chinese astrological signs the dragon is the strongest, most ambitious, most driven. Of the five sub-categories of the dragon, earth, water, wood, fire and metal, metal is the one that is most difficult to break. Geoffrey Boycott is a metal dragon in life and in his chosen profession. He makes no differentiation between the two. Life is sport, and sport is the best way of living and learning.

His own professional successes and experience have served to strengthen this conviction. He learned early that life has winners and losers and that 'winning is a hell of a lot better than losing'. He believes that the discipline that was a natural part of his early life, both at home and in school has been absolutely crucial in his professional development and performance. He regrets what he regards as declining standards in sport, education and life generally.

Never having felt the need to court popularity by playing to the crowd, other than by displaying his proficiency, public response has not influenced his direction. For many he has always had an air of self-possession that detaches; a confidence that threatens; a focus and sense of purpose that intimidate, a tenacity, dedication and, worst of all, a talent – characteristics which can infuriate as easily as they inspire. It is that certainty, that rightness, which is frequently identified as the Yorkshire characteristic by others. It is known locally as being 'brussen' in the only part of the country that acknowledges, accepts and names it.

This façade, for that is what it is, leaves little room in others' perceptions of him. It gives no inkling of inner thoughts or feelings. But be assured they are as powerful in the reflective Boycott as in any other. The dispassionate veneer masks shifting emotions, as a capricious change in

Shaw Lane in the 1950s from the left Michael Parkinson, Dennis Thornley, Barry Stewart, Eddie Ledgard (wicket-keeper), Barry Walters, unknown, Russell Bostwick and Dick Wilkinson. *Dick Wilkinson's Collection*

the weather destroys his planned strategy for batting. His strength of purpose shakes a little as first light offers the chance to see the day. Tenacity and intention go out of the same window he looks through, as he assesses whether the ball will turn, jump or seam. He needs a new plan in his head before he walks out to the crease. It is quite a revelation to share the uncertainty behind the iron mask of the man of steel; to understand the implications and feel the tension, when I had previously thought it had just rained in the night. It is interesting too for me to hear from him whom he admires from Barnsley. Paul Sykes, because he started from nowhere and made himself one of the most successful businessmen in the UK; Michael Parkinson, because he does what he does so well, knowing that he is less important than his guests. No cricketers or even sports people, I note.

On being pressed to consider success further afield than Barnsley, he spontaneously lists his own greats: Bedser, Trueman, Statham, Wardle,

Locke, Underwood, Willis. Tentatively, wary of revealing my own poor knowledge of his beloved game (despite having spent most of my childhood within a stone's throw of the great Shaw Lane), I ask if they are not all bowlers. With a brief nod indicating the affirmative, and possibly that I had got away with it, he adds Evans, and Knott to the list. I wonder still at the relevance of that off-the-cuff listing. The people to whom he pays instinctive homage are those who challenged him directly as a batsman. They were the real obstacles in his every quest to beat himself and his own previous best.

It is of little relevance to Geoffrey Boycott that he was not loved in the way some populists are. He was respected, admired, envied and sometimes feared as a batsman. No critic of his performance was ever greater than he was himself. I remember the amazement of many, in the 1970s when Boycott withdrew himself from selection for the England team. The reason was that, by his own standards, he did not warrant a place. Arrogance or downright humility? The eye of the beholder perhaps. The problem with integrity of that order was relative merit. There were people still in the team, who were not in his league, and never would be.

The line-up to be one of the elite who had bowled Boycott out was long. David Sugden recalled for me a day when Geoffrey Boycott returned to a local pub for a charity match near his home village. Boast on boast, and bet on bet preceded his arrival as the lesserlings dreamed noisily of getting the Englander out, thus securing their own place in local folklore. Hour after hour, following the actual game, he stood at the wicket putting the ball anywhere he liked until every aspirant in the crowd had had a go. Only then, with a terse nod, he packed up and left.

I would not translate that as exhibitionism or 'clevering-off' as Mrs Boycott would have said. Rather I see it as an opportunity for everyone there to seize and share a moment to take and add to their personal store of memories and magic moments. An attempt by Boycott to offer them the electrifying buzz of playing with or against a top-liner, a world-class player.

He knows that sensation, it has given him some of the greatest moments of his life, playing and out-playing the best in the world. The feeling, according to him, is worth everything it cost to achieve it. His eyes tell you that it stirs his soul in a way that he has no words for. Equally stirring but not commented on by Boycott, must have been the decision of the selectors following the Test Match against India at Headingly in 1967. His score of 246 not out was the highest – and he was dropped. My son asked his mentor and grandfather how, why and could England still win? Packing his Erinmore Mixture into his pipe with the middle finger of his right hand my Dad studied his response. 'I think there's more than one game on, lad, but while ever they've got Boycott in there, they're in with a chance.' Never a gambling man, Benny Robinson closed the discussion, Boycott was the one cricketer everybody knew they could bet their mortgage on.

Geoffrey Boycott is not an easy man to read. He has no need to be and no intention of being. As adroitly wary in our conversation as at the wicket, his initial response to my request to include his achievement as a sporting role model was typical. 'I don't even know who or what I am myself, let alone help you to use it to motivate others.' I am reminded of that lone golfer unready for public scrutiny of a skill not perfected in his view. More than most, in his life he has had the experience of feeling the sting of misrepresentation, and learned the need to avoid the slings and arrows and sheer injustice of it all. I am reminded of the oriental philosophy that every man is, in fact, three men: the man he thinks he is; the man others think he is; and the man he really is.

When I ask what, if any, regrets he has, he is unequivocal – only a fool or a liar goes through life with no regrets. It is clearly important to him to be neither, it is not how he was brought up. Pressed to identify one,

Geoffrey Boycott and cricketing history, August 1977 Headingly, 100 centuries in Test Cricket. *Patrick Eagar*

he gives the wry rare grin. Just suppose he had followed the alternative route that was open to him, University even Oxbridge he might have emerged as softer and more polished. Might he then have been regarded, in those circles where that consideration appeared to be a priority, to be the obvious first choice as Captain of England?

Much more to the point for him is to recall the greatest moment in his life. No hesitation, no question, 1977, Headingly, scoring his hundredth century in a Test Match. All else pales in comparison for him and for all the others who still say, I was there. Englishmen at Agincourt, like Marshall Litke who re-plays the moment for the thousandth time and with commentator precision describes the scene etched in his brain, when Boycott played the ball from Chappell to the boundary and made cricketing history.

Litke tells me three times the actual crowd of twenty thousand, now claim to have been there on that day, and have probably wished so long that they actually believe it. They were perhaps in Dewsbury from where, I'm reliably informed, the cheer that went up could clearly be heard. He is just another cricket lover who remembers those glorious Yorkshire days when anyone arriving late at Headingly would say 'Morning, how many has he got?' Everybody knew who 'he' was. It was Boycott, Geoffrey Boycott, Yorkshire and England, for whom the dream came true.

10
David Sugden

Pro-Vice Chanceller

The last principal of Bretton Hall College of Higher Education and Pro-Vice Chancellor of Leeds University was born in Upton, which is the wrong side of Grimethorpe, but for which he could have claimed Barnsley by birth. Other qualifications, however, have ensured that he is Barnsley by association and achievement. His education was at Hemsworth Grammar School, where he learned and was taught the educational value of sport. Upper school contemporary was one Geoffrey Boycott, already acknowledged, and representing the school, as an accomplished and dedicated sportsman.

In true schoolboy style, the young Sugden was fired by Boycott's example and his own enthusiasm and talent were recognised and nurtured by the then Head of PE Les Tate. Both accepted from the earliest days that sport would be his main interest, and suspected it would be at the cost of academic achievement. His earliest memory of success was his selection for the South Yorkshire Schoolboys' Cricket Eleven. The all-rounder tradition of the school however also led him to selection as reserve for the England Boys' Rugby Team. He literally played his way through school sportingly achieving, academically surviving but under-achieving in terms of his true potential. The buzz for him was always in the context of a sporting success.

Inevitably he played Rugby throughout his schooldays, and at Loughborough University training unsurprisingly as a PE teacher. His entry into the teaching profession was assured with qualifications in P.E. and History. For more than three years he was happy to teach, but realised he had not stretched himself. Expanding horizons led him to California and a Masters Degree at UCLA.

One of the key talents common to the best teachers, is that they never stop learning themselves. David Sugden's carefree move to UCLA put him in contact with the man he credits as having really opened his senses to the world of teaching and learning. The commitment to Rugby, he was now playing for the UCLA team, was replaced by the urge to develop the academic potential identified by his new mentor, Professor Jack Keogh. He was inspired by Keogh's vision and began to work alongside the great man in the field of specific learning disorders. His research was strengthened by his own sporting talent and teaching experience as he became involved in work linking movement and learning difficulties.

David Sugden playing rugby in California as a student. *David Sugden's collection*

Practical work with individuals and groups of children followed, resulting in a range of programmes for movement activities to combat motor impairment. Calming and relaxation techniques for hyperactivity, stimulation by the use of music and physical education activities, and all the subconsciously stored input from previous experience and learning now began to fit together like a jigsaw. One of Keogh's great strengths was his ability to identify a small group of four or five like minded bright young things and bring them together. Shared interests, equal ability, enthusiasm and competitiveness did the rest.

The Masters Degree completed, it was as inevitable as his previous path into teaching that Sugden would move on to do a Doctorate in Philosophy. Keogh's support fired him to look further into the world of specific learning disorders. Birth to childhood motor development increasingly fascinated him, appealing to the kind of response in him to provide answers, like Boycott's reaction to bowlers who got him out. It became, as it remains, his passion.

Throughout the period of research he worked with schools, individuals, and groups, practically implementing his philosophy. His experience in the field of Dyspraxia earned him increasing recognition, and he was able to support his studies lecturing. He still played the occasional game of rugby for California in Australia and in New Zealand, but the shift was now increasingly towards practical implementation of his academic research. Concentrating on seriously disadvantaged areas, he developed parental involvement in partnerships for progression for youngsters. He worked with Downs Syndrome, Clumsy Children, Cerebral Palsy and those so damaged they could not move at all.

It was totally absorbing and an incredible wrench when Sugden moved back to England in 1977 to take up a post in PE at the University of Leeds. In the years leading up to the Education Act 1981 there was an increasing awareness in schools, and LEAs, that all was not right in the world of special educational provision. The old system of a Remedial Department, facilitating the withdrawal or removal of less able children from main stream teaching, was seen to be out-dated and unacceptable. The growing realisation that modification of approach, technique, resource and overall provision for such children was leading to initial teacher training and in-service courses to include individual or special educational need as a part of the programmes of study.

Academically qualified and practically experienced, Sugden exploded onto the West Yorkshire Education scene with passion and panache. He was a practising specialist, and that was exactly what parents, schools and children knew the situation required. It was a perfect backcloth for his Cascade system of inter-action, and success followed upon success. His view, on the rights and entitlement of all children to full curriculum provision, was increasingly facilitated by subsequent legislation and development in the 1980s up to and including the National Curriculum and policies of inclusion.

The awarding of grant funding and National Health Service support for the scheme enabled the setting up of a programme for schools in Leeds and York identifying eighty children whose needs could be addressed by the system he introduced. Ongoing input, re-assessment and re-evaluation followed referral and the outcomes were of a high order. Sugden having by now become first Dean of Education at the University of Leeds, then Head of the School of Education, was in an increasingly effective position to further partnerships links with outside institutions, such as

Family and University history, The Pro-Vice Chancellor of the University of Leeds presents her degree to his daughter Rachel. *David Sugden's collection*

Universities in Europe, USA, Canada, Brazil, and back in the UK, at such places as The Dyscovery Centre in Cardiff. As a Fellow of Physical Education Association UK he was invited to present the prestigious Fellows Lecture in 2001.

His multi-professional, cascading and inter-active style, practice and experience were doubtless a contributing factor that led to his appointment as Pro-Vice Chancellor of Leeds University with responsibility for staff, promotions, discipline and grievances. His personal favourite task in this post was being the first Pro-Vice Chancellor ever to present his own daughter with a degree at the graduation ceremony. Clearly his other achievements in that role are what identified him as the ideal candidate for the role of Acting Principal of Bretton Hall in 2000, to organise the impending merger with the University of Leeds, following the departure of the former management team.

Taking over an institution of its size and history, without a single member of the original management in place, must have presented as big a challenge as David Sugden had ever faced in a scrum, or a school in all his life. Morale was low, staff exhausted, trust non-existent; this promised to be the least rewarding experience of his life. It was his personal style, open and accessible, proactive and listening, problem-sorting, straight forward, unflappable energy laced with humour and integrity, that brought the sea-change, and a successful merging of the two institutions. If you ask David Sugden whether it was good to have a toe back in Barnsley he will tell you he felt he always had, and still has, at the University of Leeds Bretton Hall Campus, possibly the most beautiful in the entire country.

11

Joan Booth

Professor of Latin Language and Literature

It's still being told, the old bar-room story, origin unknown, of a young barrister origins unknown, who was representing a Barnsley man on a charge of handling stolen goods. The judge allegedly commented, 'I trust your client is familiar with the principle *nemo dat quod non habet*?' 'No one gives what he does not have'. That isn't the joke, the punchline is the barrister's riposte 'Indeed, m'lud, they speak of little else in Barnsley'.

Since Latin is now rarely taught in state schools it would hardly be surprising if few towns, north or south of the divide, could boast alumni skilled in it. So it was a pleasant surprise to hear from Alan, the informed, chatty driver on Globe's coach from London to Barnsley, of the appointment of a woman from Cudworth as a Professor of Latin in one of the most prestigious universities in Europe. The historic Chair of Latin Language and Literature at the University of Leiden, in Holland, dates from the foundation of the University in 1575. It has never before been held by an English scholar, or by a woman.

On 16 May 2003 preceded by the Rector Magnificus of Leiden University, formally supported by Professor Averil Cameron, Pro-Vice Chancellor of Oxford University and Professor Barrie Hall of the London University, and Guy Lee, Emeritus Fellow of St John's College, Cambridge, amid historic pomp and ceremony and in the presence of His Excellency the British Ambassador, Joan Booth's slight figure, in the black velvet robes of a Dutch Professor, made the traditional walk through the crowded Groot Auditorium of the Academiegebouw to deliver her 'oratie,' or inaugural lecture.

Professor Joan Booth May 2003 arriving to deliver her oratie in the University of Leiden. *The author*

If acceptance is measured by the duration of applause following the speech, I can testify to the fact that Joan Booth's went down a bomb. I found it a unique experience. Powerful, persuasive, provocative, erudite, personal, witty and deftly delivered in English with smatterings of Greek, German, French, Italian, Welsh, Dutch and a good deal of Latin. She makes Latin sound as musical as Italian, and I understand why it was such a dead-weight subject at school for me. The experience showed me that lovingly lyrical treatment brings this dead language vibrantly to life.

My own view of the speech is validated by the general reception. Seated between the encircling ranks of gowned professors, and behind the dignitaries, are rows of family, friends, colleagues, students and members of the public, who are entitled to witness the occasion. Like Mexican waves, ripples of laughter work their way through the chamber, as translation of Latin follows quotation of the original for the benefit of those of us who need it. We have fifty minutes of learning, laughter and tears on seriously uncomfortable ancient pew seating that no one wants to leave, or even seems to notice.

The following formal reception is informal after presentation to the new Professor of Latin, and dignitaries mingle with the rest, exchanging memories, gratitude or praise beyond conventional politeness. It's a wonderful cross-section but reflects the woman herself. I am then, totally unsurprised, but delighted, when Averil Cameron tells me that, when not in formal academic dress, she wears Susan Woolf's designs. I wonder if it's a first for a Pro-Vice Chancellor of Oxford. Aunt Marion chats to everyone, and teachers and mentors as far back as schooldays reminisce. Gloria Gunson, her first role model, persuaded Joan Booth to think beyond becoming a Latin teacher, predicting the demise of linguistic Classics in Comprehensive Schools. Her parents were happy to support whatever she chose to do, though Norman Booth always suspected it would be something literary.

Acceptance by less accomplished children at Primary School had not been easy to win for a girl who, self-taught, could read at the age of three. The increasing academic demands upon girls at Barnsley Girls' High School appealed more. The work and the results brought satisfaction, and she found choices and prospects opening up. She chose Classical languages not only because she

Norman Booth celebrates his daughter's success. *The author*

loved the subject, but also because she wanted to excel at something difficult. Moving to Bedford College, at the University of London, she found herself in the company of like-minded students, in an ethos of shared cleverness, in a new group, each of whom was capable of admiring the success of the others without resentment or ill-natured competition. She found that atmosphere together with the input of her tutor, Professor Frank Goodyear, to be the right stimulus for her subsequent achievement. She says she was at first terrified of him but he was a major influence, telling her then that she had the ability, intelligence and temperament to climb to the very top. He put it down to Northern hardiness, but she acknowledges that she would not be where she is but for him. Her first in Classics helped her win appointment to a lectureship by the University of Wales, with subsequent promotion to Senior Lecturer, and eventually, due to her research, to the more prestigious position of Reader. After six years in Wales she had additionally received a PhD. One of the examiners of her London doctoral thesis, Professor Ted Kenney of Cambridge University, was to become another crucial mentor, to whom she paid tribute in her oratie for his patience, wisdom, learning and kindness.

She brought her father to Swansea to join her after the death of her mother, whom they had both adored. From there, demand grew, with her lectures heard and her research becoming known from Cambridge to Switzerland, from Montreal to Tallahassee, home of Florida State University. In Britain she became an external consultant for the Open University and its Assessor of course material in Latin, whilst promoting existing links with Mannheim, Swansea's German 'twin city', and developing new ones with Spanish Latinists. It was, however, the publication in 1991 of her highly acclaimed work on Roman love-poet Ovid, which had started to bring the recognition she clearly deserved. It amazes me to learn that she changed her own view of her ability at that stage, and never before. She appears to be a classic example in the other sense of a woman in a man's world, initially conditioned by the expectations of those around her that she would be a safe pair of hands, but not a potential mover and shaker or climber of the ladder of power and influence.

Her published works on Latin love poetry and her research activities have won her international acclaim, which will doubtless be enhanced still further following the publication of her next book on the love poet Propertius. Her early school and college mottoes, 'to search for truth' and 'to be rather than to seem', were themes of her oratie, and, I feel, reflect her own life and philosophy.

I scarcely know her, but I share the pride and pleasure of those who do when Sir Colin Budd, HM's Ambassador to The Hague says, 'I sense the drive and determination that have brought Professor Booth from a relatively humble start to the highest academic level, as shown in her appointment today. I am proud to have been here to witness a reception which is wonderfully clear recognition of her achievements and which gives well-deserved credit to a woman who is a tremendous role model, and not only for the town of Barnsley'.

Her advice to children in Barnsley is, 'Never be satisfied with less than the best you can do. Make up your mind, and even if your goal seems exceptionally ambitious, go for it'. Though their paths have been very different, she expresses a similar view to Geoffrey Boycott's in that she chose not to have what others thought of as 'fun' as a teenager, preferring to concentrate on what she knew she enjoyed, and at what she was successful. For her, the love was not cricket, it was Latin poetry. Driven by it then, she sometimes feels now that she would have liked to have a family of her own, but 'Really' she says, 'that is not a big deal; I have a wonderful, fulfilling life, and my books and my students are my legacy'. Her last word on the example she herself has set, is to quote Geoffrey Boycott. When under attack for his style, rather than his performance, perhaps by some unable to come to terms with their own mediocrity, his terse reply was, 'Just let 'em look at that scoreboard.'

12
Joanne Harris

Author

I don't believe there's such a thing as an ex-teacher, either you are one or you are not. It's like freckles, there for life. Joanne Harris is a teacher, I knew it the first day I met the post-graduate trainee. She knew it even earlier, as a child, she determined she would go to Cambridge, she would be a teacher and she would become an author. She has done all three with remarkable success, and with the same quiet determination she enjoys that success whilst rejecting the aspects she does not enjoy. She refuses to wear the labels, ex-teacher or Barnsley author. Unlike children's books with split pages to mismatch a giraffe's upper body to a crocodile's lower half, she feels no inner division being half French half English. 'Why should I? I've spoken two languages all my life. As for Barnsley, I'm too me to morph into a different accent or persona everytime I go to France or come back to England. I've never heard anyone ask Ray Bradbury why he doesn't live on Mars. Being Barnsley is not an issue for me, I'm happy with it though it is seen as a limiting device by some'. She feels moving would not be practicable since it would involve leaving the rest of the family, taking the cats away from the house, and Kevin away from Barnsley Football Club.

Her English grandfather is her urban hero, who lived to his own rules, and in time, made his dreams come true. He taught her that happiness is satisfaction of purpose, and that is the most success you should hope for. A damaged hand brought retirement from mining, opening a little shop, and having an allotment.

He had always thought he would be a gardener but wartime demands returned him to coalmining and put a hold on the dream. Her childhood falls easily into memories shared with him and in Brittany with her mother's family. There are no cupboard doors hiding skeletons in her recollections, as she describes all her family with perceptive, powerful observation and unblinkered honesty. It is doubtless from her father that the quiet gene comes into play, her mother is the French teacher who transformed learning for Jenni Murray and gave her own self discipline to her daughter. Not overtly affectionate, in Barnsley fashion, they are a strongly bonded and essentially unified, if diverse family of individuals. As with us all, it is the third generation that brings celebration of loving and being loved. She says it was having her daughter Anouchka, that growed her up.

She met her husband, Kevin, when they were like minded 6th formers. Their instant rapport before realising they loved each other is still the back bone of the relationship. They inter-act seamlessly with an empathic awareness of each other's needs and priorities. He is the supportive organisational mind, managing half of the partnership, and she is empowered in her creativity by that. They grew up together, but it is clearly more than ageing and staging, they are symbiotic. There is no competiveness, the goal is shared, and she claims his question, 'why don't you write about something you like as much as I like football?' was the idea behind *Chocolat*, making him the Beckham to her Van Nistelroy. I think he might be behind *Blackberry Wine* too. Ready for drinking now, he is also vintage, and will age very well.

They only wanted more space somewhere quiet, not a big and beautiful house, but felt they belonged the moment they walked into the house that is now their home. They had not intended to buy four acres, a leaking roof, a total re-wire, and new floors throughout. He is the site manager, of the mammoth operation but is relaxed and charming as he offers coffee. Trying to recall which toilet is working and stepping over gaps in the floor she seems oblivious to it all. Stresslessly she sympathises with my trivial concerns about my deadline. Only later do I discover that she has three herself, including her first screenplay for *Coastliners* and a diary of international commitments that would fell a PR team of six.

Joanne Harris with the man described as her urban hero, her grandfather, Edwin Short. *Joanne Harris's collection*

Success is better in your thirties, she thinks. Her twenties were the buffer of time she needed to be able to cope as she does. She is unfazed by all the celebrity and acclaim. It is rewarding in itself not to have to write for financial gain, and she has what she wants out of life in that respect. Nor does she have a mission in presenting the case for her women, who are, she hopes, the antithesis of mundane, modern heroines. Hers have to interest her first, then us, and we can love them or hate them, either will do. There are no airheads and intentionally no coarseness, though they are sensual and tempting. She takes a lack of research in writing to be arrogance, and undertakes it thoroughly, but allows that fiction comes easily to her. Even as a child, she recalls, she had a vivid imagination and the ability to concoct stories readily. Fiction can be real, but only if the feeling is genuine.

Being recognised in Tesco isn't fun, especially if one is in a mad rush, but there is an upside of recognition. It can mean invitations to No. 11 Downing Street, meeting the Browns and Cherie Blair, or better still Bob Geldof, being able to take Anouchka to the film set of a Harry Potter

Book-signing has become a part of Joanne Harris' life. *The author*

movie, meet J. K. Rowling and have Graham Ovenden paint a portrait of her. A designer dress for the Oscars ceremony, plus seeing Dame Judi Dench nominated for playing a character you created, is also immensely rewarding. Perhaps the biggest buzz happens as we talk and she opens her mail to find a gift of a signed poster from her ultimate hero, Ray Bradbury. She is ecstatic.

Her life offers more choices now, some are easy, but some are not. Becoming involved in projects with which she is in sympathy is demanding, but is a yes. Putting up with two-tier people is a no. She accepted the restructuring of characters in the filming of *Chocolat*, but will not allow herself to be reconstructed. She is not prepared to have the expectations of others imposed on her or on her writing. 'Because you ask to be taken as you are, it is easy to believe that people will do so, but it is not the case'. It is easy to be adapted by the media she finds, and is also aware of the inherent need in people to first create and then destroy heroes, and heroines.

She sees disadvantage, even adversity, as an effective spawning ground for motivation, and even high potential achievement. 'Nerdy, fat, bespectacled, anarchic people really have something to fight against; we all work harder for the things we are not given free. Being taken under someone's wing before you can fly free is not motivating, and expectations are a curse.' She is convinced and convincing. She puts me in mind of a box of her own confections, without the slip of paper guiding you to which centre or flavour will delight or surprise you next. She is sweet-smiling, young and fresh-faced, patient, friendly and responsive. The box is multi layered so intelligent, assiduous, professional, astute, provocative and inventive flavours with hard centres are in there too.

I think I know more about her now I have read four of her novels. I don't. She is mischievous too, and her amusement is patent when I ask how much of the sensual, law-unto-herself, free-spirit Vianne is Joanne. 'About half,' she says, and I nod having guessed that much. 'But I'm as much the priest as I am Vianne'. That's when I remember that it took an entire film crew, and Juliette Binoche, to create a picture of a woman that's inside this one's head.

13
Arthur Scargill

President of NUM

Half his family roots are in Ireland, the other half, traced back to 850 AD are in Scandinavia, making Arthur Scargill a Viking, possibly even a Berserker. That could explain why his raids on the political establishment have been so devastatingly historic. Unremarkable in his early years he was influenced first by his coal miner father, who had strong views on socialism and the souls of men. It was however *The Ragged Trousered Philanthropists* which first struck a textual chord for him. For me it was Oscar Wilde's view 'the best among the poor are never grateful. They are vengeful, discontented, disobedient and rebellious. Quite right to be so.'

Scargill did not immediately strike me as any of the above when I first met him. His canvassing to stand for election as a member of the local co-operative society's board of directors did though instantly strike me as articulate, strategic, intelligent and showing great potential. Asked by an independent journalist Peter Goodman, subsequently the respected Deputy Editor of the *Sheffield Star*, to recommend someone to speak on behalf of miners in a radio debate, I had no hesitation in recommending Arthur Scargill, then an NUM delegate at Woolley Colliery. The fee for that, his first broadcast he contributed to the Miner's Disability Fund, reasoning that he had taken part, as a miner so the fee was rightly theirs. In these early days Scargill was encouraged and guided by the then Branch Secretary, and local football referee Goff Sunderland.

They were more than a union, they were and remain a brotherhood that could only be irreparably damaged by scabbing, black-legging, working during a strike. Tradition dies hard in such areas and there are families still riven apart from the 1926 strike, let alone the 1984. But friendship, loyalty and kinship were equally invincible. If there was an accident underground men would routinely risk their own lives to rescue, or if that failed, to recover the bodies of their colleagues, just as servicemen would in the field of battle. Mining was a reserved occupation, requiring men to remain working underground during World War Two depriving many of what they saw as a right and duty, joining the armed forces and fighting for their country. In recognition of this the Edward Medal was awarded to men for bravery of the highest order underground, in the same way that the George Cross was awarded to civilians. It was for such men as these and their families, that the National Union of Mineworkers had

The Edward Medal, subsequently the George Medal, was awarded to Sydney Blackburn for his bravery in the Barnsley Main Disaster of 1947. Still commemorated by the families of recipients and the Royal Family, here at the ceremony in Westminster Abbey in May 2003 are his daughter, Wendy Scargill and Doris Blackburn, who was married to his brother Sam Blackburn. *Doris Blackburn's collection*

been founded originally, their growing militancy being their shield for scars from early exploitation.

Arthur Scargill's rise to become the longest serving President of the National Union of Mineworkers, is well-enough chronicled and with the impending publication of his autobiography requires no further input here. His original purpose as I recall, was to improve the health, safety, working conditions, remuneration and status of men in an industry that still fitted Wilde's description of being 'uncongenial, unreasonable and degrading.' His strategy was well-researched, high-profiled, unconditional and unflinchingly delivered by oratory rather than debate. It is rare to see anyone able to move the crowd as much as he, but Nigel McCulloch, then Bishop of Wakefield, did it. Speaking to a massive crowd in Barnsley town centre at the time of the impending closure of all the pits in the area, on the effect that the policy would have on the community, he put the Church on their side.

Miner George Porter, former W.W.I Army runner with his trophies before becoming the trainer of his niece Gloria Goldsborough Empire and Commonwealth medalist. *The Goldsborough family collection*

I think Scargill invented spin, and with passion spun webs of history, philosophy and initiative that were an inspiration to the growing ranks following tunes and brass bands like World Champions Grimethorpe Colliery Brass Band, in the annual demonstration marches through the towns of the coalfields in the North in the 1970s and 80s. Pit banners were carried by strong men, with blue scars on their backs caused from working bent double, now striding upright with emerging dignity, cheered on by healthy children, wives and mothers, proclaimed the improving working conditions and quality of life year by year. The older, used men, like Tommy This and Tommy That, smiled at the happier scenes and paraded their grandsons in pushchairs holding on to the tassels of the banners, implicitly signalling a readiness in this new generation to follow in the footsteps underground as well as in the march. The days were gone when mining families sacrificed anything and sometimes everything just to keep their next generation out of the pits. 'No lad of mine is going down a pit, I've seen enough with his Dad,' had been the extent of maternal ambition and vicarious intention for long enough. There was pride in this trooping of the colours of an industry that had long played its part in warming the nation.

Had Scargill shrugged off the mortal coil in those promising days, he would for his contribution to the industry, doubtless have been nominated, at branch and national level, for canonization; but he rode higher on Marlowe's wheel of ambition and was brought down. He had no lack of confidence and was never confused by facts once he had made up his mind. He was and remains the personification of the unsought ability, given to some of us, either to get into people's hearts and minds, or right up their noses. He has something of the Tommy Atkins who 'don't obey no orders unless they is is own,' bred in him.

He is an authority on, and is fascinated by his predecessors in the industry, and in particular their exceedingly good contributions to local folk lore. With pride, or amusement, he reports an occasional, distinct lack of finesse. First to come to mind, and I suspect, one of his own favourite stories is Herbert Smith's two-word response to Prime Minister Stanley Baldwin's proposition to the miners during negotiations in the General Strike of 1926. As a cousin of the quotable wordsmith Rudyard Kipling, and an old Harrovian to boot, it is not inconceivable that Baldwin anticipated a slightly more considered or perhaps eloquent response from Smith than, 'Nowt doing'. He didn't get it. The triple president of the Yorkshire Miners' Association, Miners Federation of Great Britain and the International Miners' Federation, kept his counsel as well as his head having little time for the gentleman ranking, and never having learned the hateful art of how to forget.

The arrival of this representative of the men who did the work for which they drew the wage at No. 10 Downing Street must rank there still as one of the most memorable ever. As the party was divested of outer

Local artist John Wood captures the moment as miners marched to Woolley Colliery through Darton at the end of the Miners' strike. *John Wood*

garments in preparation for the impending meeting Smith was told, 'I'll also take your cap sir.' Rolling it up carefully he placed it in his jacket pocket and is said to have replied, 'No tha'll not lad, ave missed caps afore, that road.' Roughly translated that would be, 'No thank you young man, but I have failed to recover my headgear on previous occasions by accepting offers of a similar nature, and have learned from the experience that it is wiser to keep it about my person, thank you'.

Scargill himself is far too schooled and too aware to play that game in that fashion, but he does allow himself perverse pleasure in recalling and re-telling it. His personal preference is for a more subtle approach in responding to what might be regarded as pretension. I believe he did his own version of it when the man who invented flying pickets was invited to 10 Downing Street for a meeting with Edward Heath, who did not care for them. On his way into the meeting for a full and frank discussion, a telephone call, designated as urgent, for Mr Scargill was received. Excusing himself he left a predictably none-too-pleased Prime Minister, accepted the call, spoke to the caller and made another call as a result of it, before returning.

Observing, as he would, the protocol of sail before steam the P.M. enquired as to the nature, urgency and priority of the call. Giving his reply, Scargill felt no doubt that this was also an area of irrevocable difference of opinion. The caller was an elderly widow, of a miner, who was having difficulty in securing delivery of her entitlement of concessionary coal, leaving her without the heating and cooking power on which she relied. Scargill's standing order in the offices of the NUM was that any on-going problems or prolonged delays in such cases should be put through to him personally. So it was. Priorities clarified, point made, the talk slid north and the talk slid south, but as history would show, without progress.

His eloquence however was not lost in the enquiries following the tragedies of Lofthouse in 1973, and Houghton Main in 1975. It was his endeavour then, and his skill in advocacy, that ensured that the proper facts were heard, and bereaved families received compensation, their only consolation.

Darton High School group visiting N.U.M. Offices Barnsley learning the history of the building from Yorkshire Miners' President Arthur Scargill 1976. *The author*

He tells me of the days when he trained to play football under the expert eye of the legendary George Robledo, in the 1940s. He asks me if I am aware that the French National Champion Horsewoman, and Olympic Equestrian prospect, Elsa Simon had her first riding lesson in Barnsley. I wasn't. He reminds me that the offices of the NUM on Huddersfield Road, were the first Trade Union Offices in the land when they opened in 1874. That made it just a hundred years before becoming the scene of the early dry rattle of new-drawn steel that was meant to change the miners' world, and did.

He is an immensely proud and complex man whom I have known personally for forty years and still do not know or fully understand. He is his own mine, of paradox, contradictions and unanswered questions. I think he might be boasting when he asks me if I remember he was voted, 'Man of the Year' in 1984, but then I know he isn't when he laughs and adds that the then Prime Minister was also voted 'Woman of the Year'.

The non-political Scargill is a rare animal, seldom sighted but worth the seeing. He is a personable, skilled mimic and funny raconteur, with a wide and wicked repertoire of personal anecdotes, often about the legendary characters he has met. They have included the Prime Ministers of virtually every country in Europe, and naturally Trade Union leaders

Arthur Scargill with Harry Belafonte and Sean Hosey in Santiago in Cuba in 1978, as guests of Fidel Castro. *Arthur Scargill's collection*

throughout the world, and names instantly recognisable, Fidel Castro, Chris Hani, Nikita Kruschev, and Yasser Arafat. With one exception, he has met every Prime Minister of England since the war including Winston Churchill. I am stunned in disbelief when he tells me who she is.

During the frenzied media cover of his every action in the 1970's urgently needing to return to London from a TV commitment in Brighton he accepted a lift from American actress Elaine Stritch. Being seen with her was no problem, but being in the back of a chauffeur-driven, pink Rolls Royce had him diving to the floor at every traffic light, to avoid the predictable outcome if he were spotted. Outside the predictable area of politicians, he quotes some of his favourite meetings with people ranging from Nelson Mandela, Diana Dors, Joan Bakewell, Vanessa Redgrave, Ian Durie, Harry Belafonte, to Billy Graham. It was the Evangelist Graham who asked him what it was that kept him bouncing back up every time the press pulled him down. 'It's called Faith, Billy, Socialist Faith,' replied the equally fervent Scargill.

He is not often given credit for being kind or sensitive, but he can be. I suspect however, that it will be for none of the above that he will be best remembered. That may well be interred with his bones, or with legions lost. For what continues to infuriate those who oppose, blame or vilify him is not so much that he always had an unswerving point of view, and was ruthless and dogmatic in voicing it; but that having stood opposed with his sling and arrows he was very often proved right, particularly in his predictions. What singularly may have contributed not only to his personal decline, but to the diminution of the NUM's role, and the end of an era of political clout, was that he was once judged as being very wrong.

During his term of office the NUM was as loud a voice and as powerful a force it had ever been. Now as his prophecies continue to come true it is divided, and stands no more in a position to change the world or its members' lives today. Revered or reviled, what is inescapably true is that for decades his face, name, voice and views were instantly recognisable across the world. His name is still as widely synonymous with Barnsley as anyone's. He is listed in *Who's Who*, and included on a CD of greatest speeches of the Twentieth Century. He is also in the *Oxford English Dictionary*, where he is now an ite, as in Scargillite.

14

Joyce Winsett

Former President of NUPE

But strange to relate there is no entry in any dictionary that I can find of a Winsettian, and maybe there should be. In the same era of the 1970s and 1980s, and in the same arena, was another trade unionist from Barnsley. Outside the TUC it may well be the case that her name, face and achievements are less recognisable. Inside the Congress no-one who was present will ever forget the frisson that went through the hall like a Mexican wave, that day in 1986 when she first stood on the platform, and told the assembled delegates to put their newspapers down and do what they were there to do, listen to the speakers.

Describing herself as 'a pox doctor's clerk', she went on to galvanise the packed hall with a presentation so individual it is still talked about today. This, recalls Rodney Bickerstaffe, was an introduction which used shock tactics to real purpose. She was not, however, intent on just shocking she had a message that she intended to be heard, and she had to break through the monotony of whole days of speeches to ensure it would be. There remains no trace of a doubt that both she and her message were heard. He defines her as typical of women from Barnsley, never flustered, prepared to tackle anything or anybody, with a great sense of humour and no shrinking violets.

If, when you are thirty-three years old and have five children aged from three months to twelve years, and your husband dies, you know that neither your life, nor theirs is going to be plain sailing. Lily Salt realised that this was the position she was left in when in 1944 her husband, Jack, died of heart failure. His heart had been weakened as a child due to rheumatic fever and years of working underground had served only to weaken it further resulting in his death at the tragically early age of thirty-five.

She had strong views about what she wanted for her children and urged

Joyce Winsett in office as President of NUPE. *Joyce Winsett's collection*

them to make the best of their educational opportunities. Fortunately, they were bright, enthusiastic and self-sufficient, but that did not make life easy. There was rationing and money was short, so short that it took all her effort and ingenuity to cope but cope she did. She bought the girls patent leather shoes, which could be made to look smart day after day with just a wipe with a damp cloth. That way she could save a few pence buying less shoe polish, which was no big deal, everyone nearby was in the same boat. The underwear the girls wore beneath their immaculately sponged and pressed navy blue gymslips, was washed every night and dried overnight ready to be worn again the next morning.

Many a neighbouring home with sparkling-clean windows behind dolly-blued curtains, and newly-scrubbed and donkey-stoned doorsteps would also have a clothes horse or fireguard full of washing, drying all night round a slow-burning fire banked up with slack. As early as she can remember Joyce Salt heard her mother saying with pride, 'My girls will have a trade all their lives'. She taught them self-preservation and self-presentation and that some appearances are deceptive, and others matter. Joyce would work to earn her pocket money, which helped the family but also helped her develop one of her strongest characteristics, independence.

It seems the child may have been mother to the woman in that Joyce Winsett also had a powerful awareness of injustice from as far back as her schooldays, and recklessness in tackling it even then. She has a still vivid memory of running from the back of the class to the front and snatching the board rubber from the hand of a teacher who was hitting another child with it. She was just ten years old. It was her first taste of representation in support of others. After a secondary modern education and Barnsley Technical College training she was one of the thousands of bright working class girls who made progress both educationally and professionally under their own steam, in an era that failed generally to recognise working class girls' abilities or facilitate their potential. Pit closures were an ill wind in many ways, but like the 1983/84 miners' strike had one very positive outcome. It united women in their opposition and their goals. Many returned to education and higher education, and Joyce Winsett was seen as being at the cutting edge of that.

She had three children by this time but with her mother's support was able to work fulltime at the town's local hospital first as a Personal Medical Secretary, then promoted to be in charge of General Administration at the GU Clinic; hence the self-applied label of pox doctor's clerk. Mentored by local councillor Mary Ryan, whom she admired immensely, she became an increasingly active member of the National Union of Public Employees. The former child who had taken a great risk in protesting at the treatment of another, also served for thirty valued years as Branch Secretary, including ten years on the National Executive

Rodney Bickerstaffe. *The author*

Committee, culminating in her election as its National President in 1986. Despite this she additionally made time for twenty one years service as a local magistrate.

No less than Arthur Scargill, Joyce Winsett walked a straight line in Trade Unionism. Her style is openly humorous and genuinely direct. Scargill and Winsett metaphorically hand in hand, and with equal panache and equal effect, were elected to the Trades Union Council in the same year. Whilst Arthur's hand in the movement may be remembered by some as a clenched fist, Joyce's would probably be the impeccably manicured finger, pointing the way. Each in their own individual way was ready to put the gloves on, or take them off, in what they both saw as a crusade against injustice or exploitation.

Joyce Winsett's TUC speech brought her to the attention of the media overnight, resulting the following year in a Channel Four documentary *A Day in the Life of Joyce Winsett*. The publicity was, however, relatively limited in comparison to the exhaustive cover given to Arthur Scargill by the media world-wide, which accounts for the fact that his name is so instantly recognised and hers is not. He was both a victim, and occasionally the ring-master, of a media circus engaged in news worthiness and hidden agendas. She never became distracted by it. Nevertheless her contribution to the Trade Union movement remains highly rated by her fellow members. Her positive style is regarded as a significant factor, in the successful merging of NALGO, NUPE AND COHSE into what is now arguably the most influential trade union in the land, Unison. Though now retired and an inveterate holiday-taker, she keeps up to date with Trade Union issues and is still consulted for her advice which is valued widely, not least by Rodney Bickerstaffe. She jokes that he has to say that because she 'taught him all he knows'. She refers to their meeting when he was but a lad, straight out of University, and she was already a seasoned campaigner. There is clearly a blend of mutual respect and great affection between the two.

It is in the genes, her instant appeal, with strong attractive features and skin as clear as her mind, very similar in approach, to her aunt, much respected, life-long member of the local Labour Party, Amelia Bailey. Like her, Joyce Winsett was born with an acute sense of social conscience, and became an active Labour party member at an early age. Together the two persuaded Joyce's younger brother, Hedley that he should also join predicting that he would have much to offer in the world of politics.

15

Hedley Salt

Deputy Lord Lieutenant of the County

He had left Holgate Grammar School early, and without higher qualification, without telling his mother knowing that she would have tried to prevent him had she known. Anyone from Barnsley knows what he means when he says she was 'sloughened' but understanding of his growing need to make a financial contribution to the household.

Hedley Salt started his working life in the Surveyor's Office at Grimethorpe Colliery. It was regarded locally as a very good job, secure and with prospects. But it was unfulfilling for the young Salt who had plans to become just that. Drawn like Kipling by the sea and the sight of salt water unbounded he joined the Royal Navy where he served proudly for nine years after training as an electronics technician with just one girl, not in a port but back in Barnsley. Sheila Warrington became Mrs Hedley Salt and he eventually decided it was time to leave the Navy, make a life back in Barnsley with Sheila and begin raising the first of their four children.

His work locally as an insurance investment officer put him right back into daily contact with local people, the silent majority. He stood for the local council in 1978, a difficult time as the smart money was on the then rapidly expanding Ratepayer contingent. He was elected on a high turnout by a narrow majority following enormous support in his campaign from Sheila and the rest of the family. He was recognised as having potential by Cllr. Fred Lunn, the then leader of the eternally predominant Labour Group. With Lunn's mentorship and that of fellow senior councillor Ron Rigby, Salt was quick to learn the ropes of his new vessel. By 1988 following the premature deaths of both men who had become not only mentors but firm friends Hedley Salt took up the offered challenge and found himself leader of the Labour Group.

He was intelligent, experienced extensively – travelled, articulate and angry. What he saw as the invasion of the local scene by national politics such as poll-capping made him even angrier. His early struggle to help support his own hardworking family had etched in his mind the belief that a state benefits system had been their salvation and sanity clause, as it had for hundreds of thousands of others. This personal experience merely served to re-inforce his professional and instinctive repugnance for another ism, that which dare not speak its name in the coalfields of the country. The Prime Minister having expressed her view that these

Grimethorpe children welcome Neil Kinnock when Hedley Salt brought him to meet them in the campaign against pit closures. *The author*

men were 'The enemy within' was enough to render Salt incandescent in his outraged defence of his constituents.

He was not, however, blind to faults and weaknesses in the traditional and rock-solid majority. During his period of leadership the local council was totally reconstructed to reduce managerial input whilst expanding the workforce. Ahead of its time the policy became a template for a score of other local councils working in similar circumstances. His trademark was straight-talking after careful listening, with a clearly-stated intention of not suffering fools gladly. He was geographically placed for it to bring success.

His retirement from the local political scene in 1995 came as a shock to the town and to the local authority. He felt after seventeen years of high pressure that he was drained of his life's energy and he wanted to give more of it and more time to his family. Returning briefly to the world of finance he then became Director of Public Affairs at Northern College, known as the Ruskin of the North, and based at the beautiful former Stainborough Castle, once home of the Earl of Strafford, a great supporter of Charles II. Hedley Salt now stands in the place of the Monarch from time to time. In 1996 he became Deputy Lord Lieutenant of the County of South Yorkshire, an office which includes deputising for Her Majesty Queen Elizabeth II on official occasions. This honour and his being made a Commander of the British Empire were in recognition of his efforts for the local community.

Following his departure as leader of the Labour group on Barnsley Metropolitan Borough Council he has worked tirelessly for the Coalfield Communities Campaign initially as its chairman. He regards the continuing success of that campaign to be as much due to the efforts of two other men as to his own. The Chief Executive of Barnsley MBC at the time was John Edwards who Salt regards as an organisational intellect of the highest calibre. Mike Wedgeworth, now a minister in the Church of England, was at the time both a Methodist lay preacher and a Labour Party member. His dual strengths were combined with a Cambridge-sharp intellect that was key in the trio's ability to work together. Mutual trust and dovetailing of skills allowed them to produce a blueprint that was taken up locally, nationally and finally at European level. They envisaged re-generation of these communities as requiring not only additional in-coming industry, but a total clean-up of the environment and a revolutionary approach in addressing the plight of local people who were losing their culture and heritage as well as their living. The continuing battle for funding has seen the decimated area benefit to the sweeter tune of half a billion pounds, in swallowing the bitter pill of punitive policies imposed in the last decade of the twentieth century.

16

Lord Mason of Barnsley

Member of the House of Lords

The man who took Barnsley as his title, The Lord Mason of Barnsley, is a member of more than one select group. First elected to the House of Commons in 1953, he remained until 1987, when he entered the House of Lords, and has now completed fifty years of unbroken active service in Parliament. It is not unique, but it is a rarity. The same could be said of him, as he remains in The House of Lords in 2003, working ten hours a day, from 9 am to 7 pm and commuting on a weekly basis between Barnsley and London. Still actively involved and with a wide range of interests could be the reason why he, and his wife, Lady Mason, working with him, look seriously younger than they are.

Work has been his life, since starting work underground at the Wharncliffe Woodmoor Colliery at the age of fourteen. He wanted to get on then, to go night school and get his deputy's ticket, as an insurance for the future. One night and one full day each week was the commitment, but without pay, and that was a problem. The pits' bonus system working five days to be paid for six, ensured regular attendance in the hard and dangerous work. It acknowledged the country's urgent need for coal, and men to dig it out, but not the benefit of incentivising education, and training. Roy Mason saw it as a short-sighted and unfair policy to many like him, having to lose the bonus to attend for day time release, and opposed it. Referral to both management and union officials brought no improvement as young miners still chose whether to lose pay or training. His reaction was to stand for election to the Yorkshire Miners' Council, topping the poll at Wharncliffe Woodmoor 4 and 5 pit.

As a delegate he worked underground, continued his studies with the aid of a TUC scholarship, and studied at the London School of Economics. Giving lectures at the National Council of Labour Colleges, he developed the art of public speaking, and as a member of the Labour Party, was soon ready, willing and able to stand again for election, this time as Member of Parliament, for his home town. With the largest majority in the country, and one of the youngest MPs in the Commons he took his seat, aged twenty-eight, and one of a new breed of NUM sponsored members. He had worked as a miner for half his life.

Wilfred Paling, the radical MP for Dearne Valley greeted him with the advice, 'If you've got summat to say, gerrup and say it.' Paling, was memorable as the man who referred to Winston Churchill in the House of Commons as a 'dirty dog,' but was instantly reminded by Churchill what dogs tended to do to palings. The new member for Barnsley much preferred the style of Tom Williams, in his view the best Minister for Agriculture the country ever had, who suggested a different approach. The wing-collared gentleman advised, 'We should look the part, be the part and observe the niceties of the House in addressing it.'

Young, but never brash, Roy Mason took the advice of Tom Williams as being closer to his own style. He also took the advice of former Prime Minister Clement Attlee, 'Keep out of the bars, and be sure to specialise.' He had literally a working knowledge of the coal industry, and had lectured on The Re-armament of Germany during his time in Education. Appropriately he identified Nuclear Energy and Armaments as significant for his future.

By the late 1950s his performance had been noted by Harold Wilson, whose view was that he hoped the Yorkshire Miners would send more Roy Masons to Westminster. In 1960 his ability to specialise was rewarded by a position as opposition spokesman on Defence. He was additionally given responsibility for Post Office Affairs, opening up a life-long interest in philately. His collection may be unique, since as a former Postmaster General in 1968, he still receives every first day cover of new issues, and then devises inventive ways of having them autographed by famous people, who are connected in some way to the designs.

With the election of Labour in 1964 he was given his first cabinet post at the Board of Trade. Promotion to Defence gave him battles of his own, as he fought the case for the Sea Harrier, from sub-committees to the Cabinet itself. 'Jump jets were fine, but at sea we needed Harriers. They had bigger engines, the newer radar equipment we needed, but they cost £70 million.' He got them. His tenacity and judgement on defence were considered sound enough to ensure a return to the cabinet in the second Labour administration.

As Minister of Power, his next move, he ensured that the Drax Power Station would not be nuclear, but coal-fired, thereby protecting jobs in mining and related industries. His defence of his former industry was powerful enough to make him tell Prime Minister Wilson that he would resign if future power policy were to be exclusively nuclear. When it was not popular to oppose CND, seeing campaigners as proposing unrealistic policies in nuclear defence of the realm, he took the decision to keep *Polaris*. He was not so much a militant, as firmly resolute in what he believed in. I wonder if like me, he saw it as a poisoned chalice when Nigel Lawson allegedly suggested him in preference to Ian MacGregor as Chairman of British Coal. I shall never know, since he just smiles.

He fought tooth and nail to locate the proposed National Exhibition Centre in Birmingham and not London. Lobbied on every side by a range of adversaries he stood firm, waiting for them, one by one, to come round to his way of thinking that regionalisation was crucial. He tells me he took the final decision alone, on the floor of the House of Commons. Having discussed with Roy Jenkins, The Chancellor, that funding was possible and that Birmingham Council was ready to support it financially, he made the irrevocable announcement. 'Please do not drop dead before three o'clock tomorrow afternoon,' was the message he received from The Leader of the Birmingham Council. He did not and his announcement was ratified ensuring the NEC was sited on an infrastructure that brought employment and revenue to the second city.

He worked to improve the geographical image of his own town, Barnsley, in the removal of muck stacks, long before Tuscany became a twin thought, and made a major input in the planning and development of the town's new hospital. But it is likely that he will be best remembered for his biggest, and last job in The Commons, Northern Ireland.

Since the posting of British troops to Northern Ireland in 1969, and internment without trial in 1971 the situation had gradually worsened. IRA bombing of mainland Britain in 1975 exacerbated the position even further. Prime Minister Jim Callagham appointed Roy Mason as Secretary of State for the Province in 1976, and changed his life, and that of his wife and family, forever. Inheriting a volatile and perilous situation, he became a prime target, and has lived in a form of confinement himself ever since. *Paying the Price*, his autobiography graphically records their experience of a life of armed guards, bullet-proof cars and loss of normality of any kind. Impromptu visits to and from friends, have gone, so have spontaneous activities since all venues have to be checked in advance. They haven't been on a train for over twenty-seven years.

I remind Lord Mason of the visit he once made to present prizes at my school's Speech Day. Rigorous advance inspection of the premises after school included the removal of some corridor ceiling tiles. Next morning brought instant, unsolicited denials of involvement from a couple of the usual suspects, which

The Lord Mason of Barnsley. *Lord Mason's collection*

merited an explanation of how the damage had actually occurred. Their outrage was refreshing, if not convincing, 'You mean Coppers did it? They want locking up, it's vandalism, that.'

Never one to stand on ceremony, he is now at the heart of the ceremonial, elevated to the peerage. A slightly reduced pace keeps him still in touch with a wide range of issues and active in the upper Chamber. A philumenist, he is President of The Lords and Commons Pipe and Cigar Club, and ignites further debate on the case for smoking, weighing the effects on health against freedom of choice. He is however unequivocal on the case for listing Chronic Bronchitis and Emphysema as industrial illnesses. Addressing their Lordships, the ex-miner put the case for expedition of recognition of the diseases, pointing out that 7000 men had died awaiting the agonisingly slow payment of compensation. In the presence of the Law Lords his comments on the potential financial benefit to plaintiffs' solicitors, would have been carefully noted.

He has come a long way and rarely been knocked off course. One famous occasion when he was rushing for the division bell in the opposite direction to Winston Churchill, he was knocked to the ground by the great man, but didn't stay down. In 1998 Lord Mason achieved victory in one of his longest running personal campaigns. Fifty three years after the war ended Bevin Boys were recognised for their contribution, and given entitlement with others who served their country in wartime, to take part in the march past the Cenotaph after the Service of Remembrance.

Though not a member of the unsurpassed Barnsley Blacks Coarse Fishing Team of World Championship fame, life could be more relaxing for the President of The Lords and Commons Fly Fishing Club, were he not otherwise involved in so many other activities. He supports a variety of causes in addition to Lady Mason's ongoing fundraising for Cancer Research. Justifiably proud of his life's work he has received recognition of it not only in being awarded a life peerage but also with a doctorate at Hallam University Sheffield, and being made a Privy Counsellor in 1968.

Politics is not a life for everyone, he believes it takes interest, zeal, energy, and hard work. As a minister he stresses, 'The policy must be your own as well as the party's. It needs to be clear that you are responsible, have good knowledge, have a safe pair of hands, and will buckle down to the job you are given.' I don't ask the retirement question, knowing the answer. He loves the work, has made five speeches in just over a year, and does all his own research, except for assistance by Lady Mason.

He has for half a century, witnessed great oratory and momentous occasions and retains a wealth of anecdotes and put-downs, together with a fascinating capacity to retell them. Before he entered Parliament, and long before it was a serious prospect, a personal interest in outer space led him to speak on 'The Conquest of Space', unsuspecting that he would one day meet living outer space conquerors, Yuri Gagarin, Valentina Tereshkova and Buzz Aldrin. During an interminally long oration the Member for Barnsley asked Ian McCleod, 'Is the right honourable gentleman listening?' to which the Chancellor R A Butler replied wearily 'Is anybody else?' Allowing the point, Mason still identifies McCleod as having admirable qualities as both man and politician. His highest respect is reserved for Hugh Gaitskell, who was godfather to one of his daughters, and whose untimely death he regards as mysterious.

The first working man from Barnsley to sit in the House of Lords is treated with no little respect himself, by both his peers and by staff there. They in turn are given 'the courtesies' equally, by the man who took Barnsley into the House of Lords, with a coat of arms and motto which reflect his former industry as well as his own life. 'Integrity and Courage.' His final words after half a century as a Parliamentarian are 'Never harbour a grudge or bear malice, do not let hate scar the soul.'

(On reflection I think I may have to reconsider withdrawing my earlier comments about Oliver Cromwell!)

17

Martin Brook

Entrepreneur

If it is not where you start but where you finish in life, then it is of no consequence that Martin Brook feels that he started off quite comfortably, as a failure. He openly acknowledges that he was a bored under-achiever at school and that he dropped out of his Business Studies Course in the first year. There was a price to pay for that self-indulgence; he has always felt that he had to work harder than those who were academically qualified to compensate for it. He also had to prove himself starting instead, a general apprenticeship in his father's quietly successful grocery supply business. He feels though, that even at that early age he was competitive and had an innate desire to win, to beat, not other people so much as problems, obstacles and most importantly his own performance so far.

His view now is that success is as much about heart as it is about brains and he had that. Mine is that he also happened to have good looks, the ability to listen and his mother's ability to charm which made him an instant success with the existing staff and customers. He liked the people aspect better than the shelf-stacking, floor sweeping and van-loading. But these tasks were not options, they were requirements to learn the job thoroughly, and in his father's view with working hard were essentials for anyone to succeed in life. It was a wise move since as well as ensuring total awareness of the trade at every level, it made him more acceptable to the work force of trusted and experienced employees. Young Brook listened hard and learnt a lot, the pay-back coming in their loyalty and hard work as the firm slowly expanded both geographically and financially as his involvement grew over twenty five years.

Before the era of the car-driven, trolley-laden super or even hypermarket, these were the days when for many the corner shop was the cornerstone of their existence in small communities across the country. In Barnsley, what was not bought in the amazing open market which had been established in 1249 by Royal Charter, was very likely bought in the corner shop. These were the retailers Brooks supplied. When the big retailing chains began to spread north they threatened not only the often cosy convenience for customers but also the livelihood of the open-all-hours little outlets. The familiar-face, sympathetic ear, enquiry about the family, pay-me-on-pay-day era began to give way to the first wave of the supermarkets' price-only matters invasions. Brooks moved with times, stepped up the personal service, spread geographically and introduced its own brand. For a while that worked, but when arrival of the real stack-em-high, sell-it-cheap foreign suppliers looked imminent, the now chairman of the company predicted that however they modernised even the larger outlets were now at risk. In the face of such progress Arkright's and the brown paper bag were history and Martin Brook decided it was time to sell up and move into something completely different – retirement.

He had invested twenty-five years of his life, and in one eighteen-month period had turned over fifty five million pounds and the dividends were handsome. He could afford to give up the pressure of business and concentrate on enjoying the pleasures of life. The good strong family ethos he had grown up with as a basis for success in life, continued with his wife Pat whose constant support was an enabling factor. He remains grateful for it as they now observe the varied achievements of their children, Jason in the family business, Julene marketing executive at *Brooklands Hotel* and Louise doing a degree in Fashion Design at Nottingham Trent.

Pat and Martin Brook at leisure. *The Brook's family collection*

Time with the family, skiing, travelling, seeing new places, playing squash and enjoying the social scene, is the dream come true for most of us. He seemed to have everything, except what he discovered he needed most, a challenge, and the real buzz of business. What he had not realised was that he had an in-built desire to achieve for its own sake, not just to convince someone else that he could. His father's real legacy was it seemed, that hard work is a necessity in life for some people, and they were such people. He had always believed that life was neither a straight line nor an automatic passage. Now he was ready to swerve off the piste and risk the relaxed and comfortable life-style for another challenge and the sweet smell of more success. Timing, and above all decisiveness were his biggest strengths.

Building seemed to be the new boom business. With the same perspicacity with which he had foreseen and temporarily outflanked the shopping revolution Brook now invested in the new scene. Sometimes in support of old and trusted colleagues, friends or customers, but occasionally taking slalom risks, he now expanded and diversified into a wide range of enterprises including the mushrooming private nursing homes. Entrepreneurial or opportunistic is in the eye of the beholder, Brook's own perception is that it was a sound commercial investment, but did not give him enough opportunity to exercise his other great strength, management of people. He adamantly believes that 'peopling' in both selection and management is the single most crucial element in business.

This people-skill that Brook has was, in part, a legacy of listening to his father whose hard work had created the opportunities he now took. Continuing to develop it he saw the benefits of using the strengths and stability of his existing team whilst engineering openings for fresh, young dynamic entrants to inter-act with them. He now applied the technique listening to his own son who found difficulty in finding variety for leisure activity in the area. Whilst admitting that he gambled on business opportunities, Brook is keen to point out that he did that only when he knew the form, the going, and the odds. Early research quickly established that the town had a population of approximately a quarter of a million people, of whom 80,000 were in the 18–30 age range. Aside from the plethora of traditional pubs, and Working Men's Clubs the town's sparse leisure facilities boasted only one night club with a capacity of 2,000. He felt instinctively that the gamble was a safe bet and went ahead opening larger and modern premises, whilst attempting to preserve one of the town's great Victorian Grade II listed buildings as the site for it

He had to stand firm in the face of six months losses having a substantial sum in the business but a year later was back doing well. Best Operator of the Year, British Entertainment Disco Association came with the now familiar pattern of geographical and financial expansion that he began to pursue, due in no small way to his knack for predicting trends. His leisure empire now extends across the UK including his personal favourite, the highly praised award-winning *KINGDOM* in Sheffield, but with twenty other popular and successful venues.

What he had to overcome to achieve that he says, was outside both his experience, and inclination to tackle. Having lived and worked in the area all his life he felt that his credentials in providing jobs and support to improve the town and its facilities were established and self-evident. His own view is that his greatest successes are outside the town because that is where the support for his enterprises was readily available in contrast to the frustration and even opposition he felt locally. He does not believe that the private sector potential in Barnsley is sufficiently valued in general terms resulting in a growing reluctance by those who could do so, to continue their efforts in making inward investment. It is a matter of regret for him that the town's location with such an excellent motorway infrastructure, should be as relatively unfulfilling and as late in development as he regards it to be. Particularly in terms of public and private sector partnership his professional experience persuades him it could be so much better.

His son Jason, looks like him, and in many ways thinks like him. As with his father and grandfather before him he has developed his own individual style and qualities, and is now Chief Executive of the Company whilst Martin Brook remains Chairman. As we take in the staggeringly beautiful view south from the M1, Brook reveals a combination of anger and regret that one of his ventures creating more than 1,700 jobs went to a neighbouring city where he found immense enthusiasm and support for the initiative. He is still passionate about his hometown and the entitlement of its inhabitants to work and play hard in surroundings of taste and quality. A recent creation to improve the environment was replacing what was originally an ice-cream factory, and became a restaurant and motel, with the four star *Brooklands Hotel*. The complex which includes a separate Health and Leisure Centre was an award winner in 2002. In addition to job creation, the offer to 4000 local people to become members was successfully if unexpectedly, taken up in the first year. Perhaps with increasing provision of similar quality all Barnsley residents will feel proud to say where they are from, rather than 'between Leeds and Sheffield.'

He points out that what he regards as pre-requisites for success in any business are the natural characteristics so often linked with the town: grit, stamina, determination, decisiveness, toughness and nous. I have a mental image of a smiling Cool Hand Luke hearing that what we have here is failure to communicate or perhaps incentivise.

Few other regrets furrow his brow. He has still the niggling thought that he did not understand the importance of education early enough, thereby making his chosen path more difficult than it might have been.

He is for me, one of the exceptions in some ways like his friend Paul Sykes and in others like former rally driver Eric Jackson. They might have all been less successful had they been constrained by a conventionally *good education*.

18
Ashley Jackson

Artist

Ashley Jackson paints the Yorkshire Moors as if they are women. To him they are serenely exciting, beautifully challenging, constantly unpredictable, and he has called them his mistress for years. Along with his family they were, and have been the biggest influences in his life. Barnsley retains elements of attraction and beauty, rooted in his memories, the people and a building, which he battled for forty years to preserve, now thought to be the town's oldest, original building.

Arriving, as a schoolboy, his name and a posh accent did little to assist his settling in with the local lads. His avoidance technique for the ridiculing he received was to use his second, and more 'macho' Christian name, becoming Norman at school, and Ashley at home. I am intrigued by the number of people, all men, to whom I have spoken, who persist to this day in calling him Norman Jackson, despite his clearly stated preference to be called Ashley. 'It keeps him in his place,' said one bravely. Unchanged, is his love of art, with a need to express it through painting. Leaving school he went to Barnsley Art College briefly before working as an apprentice sign-writer for £2.00 per week. His first role model, local commercial artist Ron Darwent, introduced the young Jackson to the Yorkshire Dales and gave him good advice, 'If you want to be an artist go all out for it, don't play at it'.

At Art School he was banned from the classroom for giggling when the live model stripped off to pose for the students. His disgrace included painting the less stimulating wrought iron gates outside the building. Reward came in the form of a young student from the commercial class, Anne Hutchinson with whom he instantly fell in love. After a five year courtship the two were married at Holy Rood Catholic Church, and the wedding was followed by a honeymoon in Blackpool. It cost the astronomical sum of four guineas a day, all inclusive, in a boarding house near Albert Road and began with a bus journey by 'Tracky'. On arrival the young couple asked the driver if he knew where their 'lodge' was, as they had the address but no idea how to find it. The driver, not aware of jobsworth mentality, insisted on taking them himself in the 42 seater bus, which finally pulled up outside the B and B.

Four days later saw them back in Barnsley, at work, and moving in to their first home. For seventeen shillings and sixpence a week they rented a private house, with a tin bath hanging outside the back door, living at the top of Dodworth Bottom. New in-laws Don and Elsie Hutchinson bought them a bedroom suite and persuaded local publican Lewis Hart, to rent Ashley a room at the *Thornley Arms* for £1 a week. Ashley Jackson had his first studio and a foot on the rickety ladder to success as an artist.

Barnsley was under-going significant change. The old hospital originally endowed by John Staniforth Beckett was undergoing partial demolition, and a larger building to replace it was being erected, a mile or so away. The nearby flower shop which had sold flowers to virtually every visitor to Becketts Hospital was losing most of its trade and closed. A Miss Haydn had the next door shop selling art materials to the students at the nearby College of Art. Ashley, who as a student there had become a regular customer, was delighted when she suggested he rent the vacant shop as a studio. She recommend him to the owner, Major Carrington, and the Ashley Jackson Gallery opened. This is the building in which Jackson takes as much pride as any work he has ever done.

Always supportive of his talent she entered one of his paintings in the local Art Society's Critic Night. He remains grateful to her and Bob Coldwell of Wilby's Auctioneers, whose purchase of his paintings was both morally and financially crucial giving Jackson confidence when the old guard of local artists did not accept him. Coldwell advised him 'If a businessman gives you the choice of his word or his bond – take the bond'. He held his first one-man exhibition in Brighouse and sold an amazing six out of twelve paintings on show.

With Anne's backing he gambled everything and took a loan from the Yorkshire Penny Bank. He painted and publicised his work with panache and flair unprecedented in the town. Even then young Jackson had the initiative to think of adorning cheques over a certain amount with, not only his signature but a sketch, so the payee had to decide whether to keep it as a collectible item, or bank it at face value. This was hutspah, the like of which was rare in Barnsley.

His paintings began to sell for fifteen shillings (75p), not enough to rent the house, the studio, and buy materials, and Ashley Jackson developed a theory he holds to this day, the universal panacea for all aches, pains and minor ailments is self-employment. In his own inimitable words, 'When you think you can't do something all you have to do is get off your arse and make the effort, and you'll find you can do it!' This philosophy, it should be said, comes from someone who has never had a grant in his life, because he never applied for one. What he did have was a passion to paint, and a family to support. With hard work and a natural flair for publicity, his paintings started to sell.

Feeling that he had reached make or break point, he submitted three paintings to the Royal Academy, which promptly refused them. He decided that if he could not get into the capital's exhibition official scene he would hold an informal exhibition of his own with the pavement artists in London. With no research, but two good mates to back him up, he set off for media-packed London, the weekend of the World Cup Final in 1966. Blissfully unaware that they needed a permit to exhibit in public, they set out his work on a busy Westminster Bridge. It could have been the location, the swelling crowd, or the disgruntled regular exhibitor next to him that brought them to the attention of a police officer, who asked if they had a permit. The old Jackson hutspah, combined with some slow-timing from drama student Jack Brown, and mate Peter Midwood saved the day.

Giving assurances that he did have a letter of authorisation, he was abetted by the other two urging him to show it to the officer. His inability to produce it together with an apparently gormless reply, 'Well I knew it was important so I put in a safe place. It's at home in the sideboard drawer,' produced tutting headshakes from the accomplices, but tolerant acceptance of his northern naivete from the metropolitan constabulary. He was allowed to stay but not to sell – officially. A BBC TV crew became aware and interviewed him for national TV on one of the most viewed weekends in British Television history in the past fifty years, and one of the most inspiring ever. Those who worship at that shrine still chant the awesome names Banks, Cohen, Wilson, Stiles, J Charlton, Moore (Capt.) Ball, Hunt, B Charlton, Hurst, Peters. My son, sang it as a lullaby to his son George. The Barnsley team of three returned from London that weekend feeling every bit as victorious as Bobby Moore's eleven.

But despite the exposure and its resulting increase in the sale of his work, expenses were in excess of income. He worked, often until midnight, sign-painting wherever he could find the work to support his water-colour painting, and provide a living. In 1969 an exhibition in Dewsbury was attended by respected art expert and critic James L Brooke. Days later Jackson received a letter from Brooke saying he had a unique talent and advising him to exhibit in London.

Easily said, expensive to do. He visited London in an old Morris ex-Post Office van, in which he also slept, using the wash and brush-up facilities in Paddington Station as his hotel. He was told, that he would need to dress in a suit to sell to London Galleries. He didn't own one, but got one, and started literally, knocking on the doors of every art gallery in London. At the Upper Grosvenor Gallery Rodney Brangwyn, who was also wearing a suit, a green velvet one, suggested that Ashley should leave his portfolio with him to show to the governors of the gallery, returning the following Monday for their decision. Doing so, he returned to hear that they had not seen his work, as they had been to Wimbledon all week, and would he come back yet again the following week?

Realising that he simply could not afford another journey, and it was 'muck or nettles', as we say in Barnsley, the Irish, the gypsy and the artist exploded saying that he could afford neither Wimbledon nor to come back again, and if they did not like his work they should just say so. But he left the portfolio and convinced that he had 'shot his bolt' returned home totally frustrated.

Three miserable days later he received a telegram asking him to telephone the gallery. The good news was that an exhibition had been arranged for him. The bad news was the he had only six weeks to prepare for it, and it would cost £3000. Despite the fact that their first child, Heather had just been born, Anne told him to put up their house as security and do it. That support was the turning point in his career, when dreams became a practical reality.

In London for his first meeting with the board of governors of the gallery, he felt very insecure and out of place. He had, by now, learned a lot about art, and even a bit about commerce, but he didn't know how to address a Duchess on first meeting one. It didn't matter as it turned out since the Duchess of St Albans, an important member of the board, just laughed when he told her, and said, 'Call me Suzannah then, it's my name.' His nerves vanished and were replaced by the exhilaration of a career taking off. He sold one third of the exhibited paintings, was featured in every newspaper and saw instantly that publicity equals sales.

If you stand on the front step of the old and beautiful Ashley Jackson Gallery opposite the Norman tower of St Mary Church in Barnsley, you can see the time by the clock on the impressive town hall. At ten o'clock on 11 October 1969 L S Lowry walked into the gallery. The cocky young artist half choked on a crisp and could not speak, as Lowry bought a sketchbook, using the time it took to wrap it to scrutinise the work displayed. He stood gobsmacked and then heard L S Lowry ask to buy one of his paintings. He must have told the story thousands of times but he still relishes every incredible word as if it happened yesterday. There is spin you can create, and situations you can manipulate, but there is no way you can sell a man like L S Lowry a painting he does not want. This was not Anne, supporting him for love, this was professional recognition that even he had never dreamed of. Like a paper towel soaking up excess water he absorbed every word the old master spoke. For Jackson, it was the moment he decided to ignore his critics and detractors in the traditional establishment of the art world and follow his own direction.

It was unbelievable, the speed with which he became the darling of the water-colour world. The times certainly were a changing. It was obligatory to wear a Quant, sit on Habitat, listen to Beatles or Stones, flutter with Biba and now to have an Ashley Jackson. He became collectible and with a wonderful twist of irony the Yorkshire Bank advertised loans to customers to enable them to buy his works. I wondered if they had any idea how many originals they had enveloped and filed in their cellars year after year.

His approachability may account for the number of people who seek his advice on water colour technique, though he gives it readily sought

Ashley Jackson and his old friend, one of Barnsley's great heroes, Brian Glover, with Bill Owen, who played Compo in *Last of the Summer Wine*. *Ashley Jackson's collection*

or unsought, even to the Prince of Wales. He is one of few people for whom Prince Charles has agreed to open an exhibition. Arthur Scargill and Patrick Duffy (or Bobby Ewing), Barbara Taylor Bradford and Kathy Staff, Ronnie Hazlehurst and Yehudi Menhuin, Liz Dawn and Nanette Newman, Tony Christie and Tony Benn, Bernard Ingham and Danny La

Ashley Jackson autographs a sketch for each of thirty one local children at a summer school at Bretton Hall. *The author*

Rue, have something in common, they have all bought Ashley Jackson's. Yorkshire Business Connection presented one to ex-President Bill Clinton, and the Royal Naval Department and the Ministry of Defence commissioned paintings. He hangs in NATO, the 2nd Parachute Regiment of HM Forces, the Yorkshire Cricket Club, British Gas and The Yorkshire Post. The opinions of ex Prime Ministers Wilson, Heath and Major were in rare harmony, on owning his work.

His one man shows, exhibitions and international cruises are too numerous to list. Coast to coast TV appearances have drawn crowds to his American Exhibitions in New York, San Francisco, Chicago, Washington and Dallas. His face has become familiar on British TV over twenty years of appearances. He has published several books and is listed in *Debretts* and *Who's Who in Art*. His name is inextricably linked with the Yorkshire Moors and will become even more so since Yale University, having acquired the rights, has chosen his work to illustrate the front cover of its new publication of *Wuthering Heights*.

He is uncharacteristically quiet showing me his other work, depicting the savagery of war, from the Falklands, to Northern Ireland to September 11th. As we move through the deceptively large upper storey of his

Ashley Jackson in his Holmfirth Gallery. *The author*

Holmfirth Gallery viewing his latest work, I ask him if his skies are softening. 'They're bloody not, the only thing that's softening is me with my grand children. They're my greatest achievement, not this lot!' I know exactly what he means.

There is nothing quite as sickening as success that isn't yours, and Ashley has had the highs of achievement tempered with the lows of resentment from others, who see his art and even the landscape with different eyes. He is as resolutely stubborn today as ever, and never fails to find something to laugh at in the world's varying responses to him. Still a grafter by nature, he is a man whose paintings sell for thousands of pounds but proudly calls himself working class.

He was unloading a lorry helping the driver make a difficult delivery to his gallery on an impossible corner in Holmfirth, when I arrived to talk to him. 'You don't mind waiting do you?' I don't want folk round here to think I'd ever get too big for my boots to sweat a bit, doing a spot of fetching and carrying,' he explained. Daughter Heather Beaver who manages his affairs, as well as being an independent television producer in her own right, made a cup of coffee for me as I waited, explaining she works with, and not for her Dad; a nice point. She grinned and nodded towards him as Ashley exploded back into the tiny gallery. 'Did you hear that? That bloke riding past on that bike? He's just shouted across that I ought to be able to afford somebody to do this for me, and called me a tight bugger. You just can't win'. That's life, well it's Ashley Jackson's, and it is rarely still.

19

Sir Thomas Elmhirst

Air Vice Marshall

Thomas Walker Elmhirst born fourth of nine children to William and Mary Knight Elmhirst, spent a happy childhood in Barnsley, believing no child could have had a better start. By that he meant discipline, happiness and privilege – but not indulgence. Toys were few and had to be cared for, spending money was one penny per week. He learned early that all were, and should be treated equally in the family and in life, which meant no favourites and no preferential treatment, an early lesson in philosophy which he applied all his life.

After boarding school, which he hated, he entered the Royal Naval College at Osborne as an 'awestruck schoolboy nervously witnessing his first gun salute'. In classes there, his contemporaries were the Princes Edward and Albert, later to become Kings Edward VIII and George VI respectively. Elmhirst claims no great talent or evidence of potential at this stage. Rated as he was, 35th in a company of 70 in academic work, might appear to support his view, and that he had no sporting skills either. His own life story many years later cites his participation in more than twenty five different sporting activities including being capped for the RAF at Twickenham. Suggesting perhaps that late development is no hindrance to success.

A posting to *HMS Cornwall* as Midshipman led to three months below decks in the engine and boiler rooms before promotion to above decks manoeuvres and big gun practice, which for him was not immediately perfected. An enthusiastic return to the family home with a souvenir cannon led to a demonstration of his professed skill. Evidence remains of his lack of it, in the form of a half-demolished fire place in the dining room.

One of twenty young officers selected by the Admiralty he trained at Cranwell to fly and captain the new fleet of hydrogen-lifted airships, which were to patrol Britain's coastlines due to the threat from German submarine attacks in World War One. Successfully making the first ever East West crossing of the Irish Sea by Airship or balloon, brought a challenge from an aeroplane pilot who boasted that he could fly his plane under the Menai Bridge. Undaunted, and admittedly emboldened by alcohol, Elmhirst responded that he could do that in the airship. Sobering up he reconnoitred the area and then achieving what everyone thought to be an impossibility, he flew the airship under the bridge. His family

The Menai Bridge escapade. *The Elmhirst's family collection*

still maintains that had his CO's, like the rest of the world, not been celebrating Armistice Day he would have certainly been court-martialled for that display of derring-do.

Training to fly aeroplanes at Cranwell took slightly less time in those days than it took my grandson Charlie to learn to ride a bike. Two hours to balance the aircraft, two hours learning to turn and two hours learning to judge the speed and height. Then solo and skyward.

By 1925 the RAF was involved, ironically, in support of the Kingdom of Iraq and Transjordan, needing information on the Turkish Forces threatening Iraq. The Secret Intelligence Service, using university dons to crack codes and ciphers, needed more practical involvement on the ground, and Elmhirst volunteered for the dangerous undertaking. Turkish co-operation followed in its subsequent neutrality, and Elmhirst was promoted to Wing Commander as Air Attaché in the Diplomatic Service at the British Embassy – in Ankara.

With the outbreak of war in 1939 he returned to London, as Duty Air Commodore. Amongst other duties he was put in charge of ordering Red Alert Air Raid Warnings. Enormous responsibility was simplified by following the family tradition of no preferential treatment for anyone. All requests for lifting the alerts were resisted, even if from the Prime Minister, Winston Churchill, the Governor or President of Northern Ireland and even the Royal Family at Windsor. His sense of 'rightness' led him at times to question decisions at the highest level, even Churchill's judgement, using his own experiences and empirical observations to support his argument.

By December 1940 Air Commodore (Acting Vice Marshal) Elmhirst was dispatched from London to Ankara, to consolidate the neutrality of

Turkey or to bring the Turks into the war as an ally. This posting was arguably in recognition of the skills he was now clearly strengthening. He proactively developed contacts to initiate networks and forged reliable links at any and every level. His success relied heavily on the relationships and the reputation he had won in his earlier work there.

At that stage he was joined by his wife Katherine and their children, Jane and Roger. Entertaining had been an important element in the building of professional relationships, and Katherine had proved stalwart and invaluable in her contribution to that. His previous contacts were consolidated and the family was welcomed with trust and warmth. Elmhirst loved the social whirl which included the company and respect of the President of Turkey, Kamal Ataturk. His respect for the President was partly due to the man's ability to drink alternate glasses of vodka and champagne for six hours and still walk unaided from the room!

Elmhirst's universal acceptance by the Turks was rooted in his understanding of their pride in being a nation which had centuries of history at war. A people who needed no explanation of bellicose strategies, Turkey chose its allies with caution, and then, only when trust had been firmly established and tested, and threat no longer existed. His personal contribution to this diplomatic courtship was regarded as crucial in both political and military terms. This was subsequently acknowledged when following Ataturk's death, Elmhirst was invited to attend the funeral not only as a representative of his country, but as a trusted colleague and personal friend.

With the Battle of Britain over in 1941 and Turkey covertly assisting Britain, Elmhirst was given command of Number 202 Group in Egypt with Arthur Tedder as Commander in Chief. They were an odd couple, Tedder finding relaxation and socialising difficult and Elmhirst living every day to the full. Tedder publicly acknowledged the role Elmhirst played at the end of the war, choosing him as a sponsor when granted the freedom of London. Elmhirst in turn, valued Tedder's support and co-operation for his initiatives as crucial, in what was widely regarded as his own finest hour. The organisation of the Desert Air Force had been described as 'an administrative mess.' Elmhirst carefully, systematically and occasionally ruthlessly transformed it into a slick, professional machine. This afforded him not only the greatest personal satisfaction in his military life, but acclaim that ranged from the ranks to Montgomery himself.

Army Commander Montgomery was even less convinced of the value of socialising and hospitality than Tedder, according to Elmhirst's observations, so entertaining was delegated to him. The King of Greece and Field Marshal Smuts were amongst the many VIP's he greeted, as was Winston Churchill, whose visit required a change of policy. Elmhirst foresaw the PM being unhappy with Monty's rule of no drinking or smoking in the mess. The Principal Medical Officer, an old rugby team mate, was prevailed upon to provide an allocation of medicinal brandy which was placed in front of the Prime Minister. Together with rare Havana cigars (a present from Katherine to her husband), the meal originally described as 'grim' was transformed, despite being normal rations, as the great man unwound and regaled the mess with countless stories.

Elmhirst's diary at this time routinely recorded contacts and meetings with legendary names. Eisenhower, whose toughness he admired, and De Gaulle whose damp handshake he did not. Alanbrooke, Alexander, Maori Coningham, Beamish, Kirton, in discussions of then relatively unfamiliar, but subsequently historic, locations Torbruk, Tripoli and El Alamein. He still however had an ear to the ground for matters of less than national significance. He was informed by his Principal Medical Officer that key men were lost to the services for periods of time up to six months due to the inefficiency of the Army hospitalisation system for them after contracting sexually transmitted diseases. His response was typically pragmatic, his solution simple. Staffing provision for a small RAF hospital in Cairo to deal with the condition quickly, efficiently and locally, enabling a swift return to duties. The plan was accepted by Tedder and put into operation forthwith.

His second suggestion that the risk of infection would be radically reduced if an official brothel were to be established in Cairo and the Canal Zone was met with less enthusiasm. Whilst seeing the relevance, no one was prepared to raise the issue with Montgomery or to approve the scheme personally. Elmhirst took the absence of an order not to proceed in the spirit of Nelson's telescopic surveillance at Copenhagen in 1801 and duly set up two such units under the supervision of the RAF's Principal Medical Officer. Sick leave figures were noticeably reduced and Elmhirst also recorded receiving requests for other serving men to use the facility from two Senior Army Commanding Officers.

Ordered back to England he undertook the organisation of the new 2nd Tactical Force for the summer of 1944. His flair for using strengths to the maximum, and refusing to accept defeat or obstruction at any level, made him the tactical and administrative genius he now was. Air Marshal Sir Basil Embry recorded in 'Mission Completed', that 'Elmhirst transformed the whole operation in a matter of weeks; having the ability to move mountains with a twitch of his bushy eyebrows.' It was this pragmatism, this giftedness for managing situations and people of any rank, that contributed to the recognition he received at the end of the war, a knighthood. And there, one might suppose, the story of Sir Thomas Elmhirst would end.

But of course it didn't. He became Director of Intelligence at Whitehall for a relatively quiet period of his life. Then, in the grip of one of England's fiercest winters in living memory, he was given the opportunity to go to India as Chief of Inter-Service Administration. The move was not without challenge and risk, as it entailed responsibility for combining the administration of the RAF and the Indian Navy in the areas of supply, organisation and medical staff. It would require the removal from their posts of high-ranking key officers. In addition to which it was in a geographical area in which he had no contacts and had never even visited. Finally, he arrived only two days before the new Viceroy of India, Lord Louis Mountbatten and his wife Edwina.

Elmhirst's diplomatic skills had never been so tested. The ongoing disputes between the navy and the military ran alongside the need to meet and establish good working relationships with the Presidencies of Bengal, Madras and Bombay and the Generals at Rawalpindi, Poona, Peshawa and Karachi. The tour he made to begin this daunting task served to highlight further the problems that lay ahead. The established ex-patriot population of soldiers, businessmen and civil servants had strong views. What they saw was the development in irrigation, railways, roads, forestry, literacy and a common language through which law and education were more accessible. What they saw perhaps less clearly, he thought, was the deprivation, the mere existence of millions on the outskirts of the ever growing cities; and most importantly the degenerative effects of dependency and dis-empowerment with the resentment that automatically accompanied all of this.

Lord Louis Mountbatten arriving in India. Second left is Thomas Elmhirst. I am unable to ascertain whether Wentworth Beaumont is next to him.

The British Government's promise that India would be handed back to the Indians at the end of the war, was in Mountbatten's brief which included seeing that this was done before Britain risked becoming embroiled in the political dispute between the then Hindu and Moslem parties. Whitehall supported Mountbatten's view that the country be partitioned with the Hindus led by Nehru and the Moslems by Jinnah.

Like Mountbatten, Elmhirst evidenced a natural ability to use charm or utter ruthlessness, depending on the requirements of the situation. Skilled in delicate negotiation but disciplined and adamant in the implementation of policy, the two, together with Mountbatten's ADC Wentworth Beaumont, who was brought up at Bretton Hall, worked in tandem through a minefield of sensitivities, feuds, entitlements, rights, empire building and egos. Elmhirst, equally liked, respected and trusted by Pandit Nehru, as he was by Mountbatten, wrote gossipy letters home, feeling that Mountbatten might be taking the pace of the handover too quickly. Subsequently leaked media gossip has alleged that Mountbatten may well have felt an inclination to depart sooner rather than later with his wife, to return to London. It would appear that Elmhirst and Beaumont completed their task adroitly skirting both personal and political issues of a high order.

Of these historic days in which he played a significant part, Elmhirst found one of the most memorable was being present on the lowering of the British flag by Mountbatten, the last Viceroy, for the raising of the Indian flag by Pandit Nehru. He was also present with more than a million mourners at the country's ceremonial burning of the body of the great leader Ghandi, whom he had known well before Ghandi's assassination.

Sir Thomas Elmhirst came to know Pandit Nehru well during his time in India. *The Elmhirst's family collection*

In August 1947, Nehru personally requested that Elmhirst become the first Commander-in-Chief of the new Indian Air Force, leaving him unable to accept a similar offer from the Prime Minister of Pakistan. The accolade was confirmed when the New Delhi Polo, Hockey and Cricket Club dubbed him further by naming the club's new pavilion after the erstwhile Royal Naval College cadet with 'no great sporting promise'.

He returned to England where he was happy but unstretched, until he received a call from the Chief of Air Staff offering him involvement in one of the most secret missions of all time. In 1952 Britain's first atomic bomb had been tested off shore NW Australia. Now the second was to be tested, on land, following extensive secret work at Aldermaston, and Elmhirst was sent to meet the mastermind of the A Bomb project. William Penney told Elmhirst he needed a man who could organise efficiently, get on with a range of people and supervise the top-secret operation to fly the next atomic bomb out to Australia for testing.

This was a mission to test Elmhirst's considerable expertise as he encountered empire building of a new order in the administrative quagmire of the Ministry of Supply. More lay ahead in the need to

This photograph of the first land explosion of the Atom Bomb in Australia in 1953 was signed and presented by Sir William Penney to Thomas Elmhirst in recognition of his contribution to *Operation Totem*. This was the code name for a mission so secret that Penney's flight to Australia was booked in Elmhirst's name. *The Elmhirst's family collection*

negotiate the minefield of diplomacy that would enable the flight of a British aircraft over European, Middle Eastern and South East Asian countries carrying an atom bomb in total secrecy. The bomb was 'successfully' exploded in Australia in October 1953.

From the original approach in January 1953 to the completion of his mission in October, two other events took place in his life. To act as the personal representative of the Monarch is accepted to be the highest honour available to former members of Her Majesty's Forces. Elmhirst's appointment as Governor of the Channel Islands, was for Her Majesty, an opportunity to hear first hand Elmhirst's account of the atomic preparations.

To be present at the Coronation of a King or Queen of England is an even rarer honour, given to one representative from each of the three services. The man chosen to represent the Royal Air Force under the direction of the Earl Marshal of England, was Sir Thomas Walker Elmhirst. The three areas of responsibility were the Abbey entrance, the choir and finally the Chancel, the Bishops and the Royal Gallery for which he was given responsibility. He was allocated twelve officers to assist him but characteristically insisted he could manage with four. He was told that since all twelve were entitled to Coronation Medals, all twelve were to take part. His own account of his duties that day is yet another indication of his ability to keep his head out of the clouds. He was to assist the ladies

Sir Thomas Elmhirst, as he tries to explain away an error in organisation spotted by the Queen on her 1957 visit to the Channel Islands. *The Elmhirst's family collection*

Coronation Day Sir Thomas and Lady Katharine Elmhirst. *The Elmhirst's family collection*

from the Blood Royal Gallery down the narrow steps into the Abbey and lay out their trains behind them; ensure that place names were on the correct seats; provide a small stool for the four year old Heir Apparent to stand on; and finally to ensure that the lavatory was properly equipped!

His greatest pleasure that day was that his position there entitled Katherine to be present too. Moving next to the Channel Islands for five years enabled them to be together privately and professionally, and time for shared interests and the re-living of memories of their exciting and sometimes dangerous life. His description of his swearing in as Lieutenant Governor of the Bailiwick of Guernsey, Sark, Alderney, Hern and Jethon completed a circle in his life. Eyes moist as when young Midshipman Elmhirst stood to attention for his first gun salute on *HMS Cornwall*, Sir Thomas heard an eighteen gun salute and the opening bar of the *National Anthem*, played in his honour.

Retirement of a sort came in 1958 when he moved to Fife, although he undertook the duties of Deputy Lieutenant for Fife from 1960 for ten years. For sixty years his life's work had taken him around the world with some of the most famous and influential characters of the twentieth century. Whilst not handsome in the conventional Hollywood sense, he was clearly a charismatic character who enjoyed the company of women, and in return was attractive to them. He had met and entertained internationally celebrated beauties such as Vivien Leigh, Bea Lillie and Dorothy Dixon during their ENSA tours of North Africa. When single, he had enjoyed a romantic interlude with the beautiful wife of an Egyptian cotton Pasha on the Orient Express (and taken up a subsequent secret invitation to visit her in Alexandria.)

But the real love and emotional stability in his life was Katharine. Through the years his letters record his need to have her with him in times of stress or diplomatic uncertainty, but also simply to enjoy a new posting together. Her input in her loyal support in meeting, entertaining and winning friends and allies was invaluable and her death in 1965 came as a terrible blow. He would not have been the man he was, however, if he had not the capacity to overcome even that. In his later years, failing in health, he was cared for by his second wife Marian, until his death in 1982. Four years later, had he lived, he would have been at Westminster Abbey again when Marian's granddaughter, Sarah Ferguson, married Andrew Albert Christian Edward Windsor.

Thomas Elmhirst was not given a fascinating, exciting life, he made one for himself. He was unable to untangle courage and foolhardiness even in his own mind, citing the Menai Bridge escapade as an example. The only times he records fear are occasions when he is responsible for, and fears for the safety of, those for whom he has responsibility. He believed courage could be taught by example or leadership, and obstacles overcome by enterprise and effort.

It is undeniably clear that he began life in a comparatively privileged position, so did thousands of others who achieved far less. It is equally clear, he never allowed privilege to become an obstacle. His lifetime contained enough to satisfy half a dozen lives in terms of duty, accomplishment and excitement. As he might have said himself, he did champion. A quite ordinary young man forged for himself a most extraordinary life, which could have been the basis of a blockbuster Hollywood film, but who would have believed it?

20
Rita Britton

Fashion Retailer and Consultant

What Barnsley is not famous for is its contribution to the world of glamour, style and elegance, it doesn't fit the image, but maybe it should. Historically financially harrowing, the Twenties and Thirties were softened, to some degree for people in working class areas, by the growth of the age of the cinema. Throughout those years, and the warring Forties, into the Fifties, Alice Robinson went to the cinema as many as ten or twelve times a week. The newsreels showed her the lives of the rich and famous wearing Chanel, Beaton and Hartnell, but it was Hollywood designers, especially Edith Head who provided an escape with opportunity to widen her vision.

With what she stored in her mind's eye, and the ready stock of fabric she always had, she went home with an idea already half-formed. Then, unable to rest until she had the finished product, she worked through the night, oblivious to everyone and everything else. By morning she had her own design of the latest styles from the silver screens of the Alhambra, Empire, Globe, Pavilion, Princess, Ritz and Star cinemas in Barnsley.

One button more or less, a lapel asymmetrically countered by a balancing hip pocket. Waists dropped out of sight, or wasp-tight; full-skirted dresses in soft pastel wool crepe with contrasting coloured linings for scarves, stoles, pockets or collars on heavy check and tweed coat-dresses. Forty tiny black pearl buttons, or one enormous one, self-covered or startlingly contrasting with the fabric. Fur trims, silk inserts, high necks, low backs, wrist to waist dolman sleeves or the subtlest hint of a capped one, sloping, sensual shoulders, or aggressively padded ones. Panels, to float with the movement of walking to reveal pencil sharp skirts or slit tunics over wide-legged, perfectly cut slacks. With no need of the paper patterns that were the vogue and salvation of the less adventurous, she designed intuitively, cut instinctively and created instantly. It was both her success and her failing. The results would create an envious demand that she could, or would not satisfy. She would have forgotten what she did, or how she did it or simply become bored by it, and moved on irrevocably.

Tiny, slim and with a natural elegance, her friend Anne Dooley did not just wear Alice Robinson's creations, she modelled them. Her daughter, another Anne, princess-dressed to co-ordinate with her mother's latest outfit, stirred receptive eyes and aspirations in the mind of her best friend, Rita England, who desperately wanted to look like that, and felt she didn't. It was all observed, logged and filed away in the back of the little girl's brain for future reference. The two youngsters watched Alice's own daughter Sybil, older than they were, develop from being an equally unpromising child into a stunning model and successful beautician. Modelling hairstyles for top stylists, first Barnsley's Lesley Frances, and then with Muriel Hampshire from Wakefield and her husband Syd (of Hampshires Commercial Hotel, Cheapside) she became a part of their triumphs winning British Hairdressing Team International Awards and honours in the 1950s. They were trend leaders as Hollywood blew the fresh air of make-up and fashions back over the white cliffs of Dover. This post war decade of women wanted to look, and feel, feminine again and turned away from uniforms and uniformity. Burning bras had not yet arrived, but the final burning of ration books and clothing coupons had, and post-war frivolity and glamour slowly arrived in Barnsley throughout the Fifties.

Sybil Robinson. *Muriel Hampshire's collection*

By the Sixties Anne Dooley was dancing out of the town to cabarets all over the globe, and her friend was drawn into a different world, the world of Mary Quant, Twiggy and Audrey Hepburn. Rita England, now better known as Rita Britton, was born in relative poverty, relative

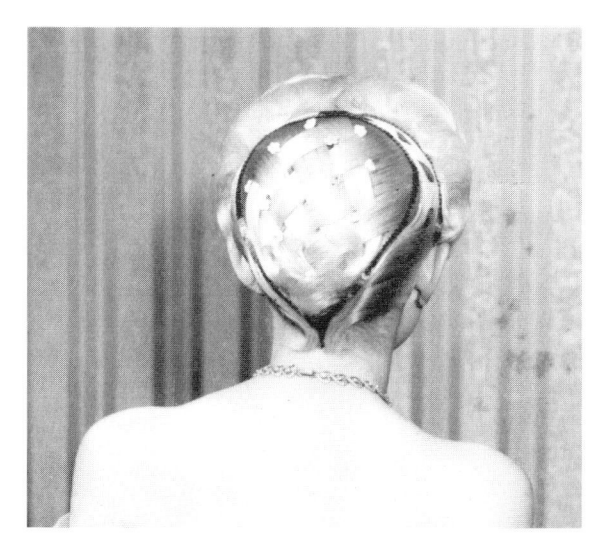

Sybil Robinson models a Muriel Hampshire hair creation. *Muriel Hampshire's collection*

Leslie Frances and Muriel Hampshire, national hairdressing team winners collect their trophy. *Muriel Hampshire's collection*

Sybil Robinson with one of the many trophies won by Leslie Frances, Muriel Hampshire and Syd Hampshire at national and international level in the 1950s. *Sybil Maley's collection*

because she was fed, loved, and cared for in the warmth and security of an extended family. So the fact that she was bathed (the a is short and pronounced as in fat) in a tin bath was, and remains, irrelevant. Poverty is only an obstacle if you are obstructed by it, as she was unaware of demographical ratings as D or E, it didn't matter. What did matter was that she was brought up to believe in herself, so in fact, she was never poor, she simply began life in a family that did not have money.

Pollyanna is a reflection of Rita Britton herself, what you see is what you get. It is a crucial ingredient in the phenomenal success of the most celebrated, visited, written about shop in the

Sybil Robinson in Hollywood style, she was a member of the first wave of Max Factor beauticians as well as a successful model. *Sybil Maley's collection*

UK, possibly the world, dependent on one woman, supported by a small team of long-serving professionals. They do not sell clothes, they facilitate the purchase of them. They seamlessly inter-act with shoppers who fly to Manchester or to Leeds Bradford, and taxi to Barnsley for the day, just to add to their collection of Margiela, Jil Sander, Jean Muir, Shirin Guild, Ben de Lisi, Alexander McQueen and more. Rita Britton, Managing Director, marketing and merchandising brain of the business, could be washing the front doorstep, waiting on table, washing up, or giving yet another interview. It is why people, who could shop anywhere in the world say they love to come to be recognised, remembered and receive the sort of personal attention they say they cannot get anywhere else. That could be why the place is regularly named retailer of the year, and why Joji Yamamoto grants it the unique privilege of being the only store in the world to offer all his range alongside Issy Mayake and Comme des Garcons.

Less is more is the essence of this place, minimal, understated and largely black, white, beige and grey. Paradoxically, it is the antithesis of Rita Britton herself who presents as extrovert and gregarious with a unique personal stamp. She is a non-occasion dresser and the only mother of the groom I have ever seen wearing trainers at the wedding. A mosaic of contradictions, she is just as happy listening to Beethoven in solitary splendour as she is sharing stories, taking centre stage, giving one of the innumerable speeches requested of her, or lining up to meet the Blairs or not lining up to meet the Majors at Downing Street receptions. She seems to thrive on pressure, an adrenalin addict, who listens as carefully as she extemporises, accepting everyone – but not everything. Multi-millionaires, sporting icons, film, stage and TV personalities chat to locals, politicians, market traders, office workers, and the senior citizens she adopts by the handful. You will find yourself sitting between plastic super-market carriers and Robert Clergerie handmade bags, owners of all greeted and treated equally. She has less pretention and more style than anyone I, or she for that matter, have ever met.

She carries her lack of achievement at school simultaneously as a scar and a banner, feeling no shame in it, but it didn't help. With Freedom of the Borough and an Honary Doctorate awarded to her, it should be academic anyway, but it is still occasionally a source of vulnerability in an otherwise skilled and confident professional. She has an ongoing passion to learn, and to work in anyway she can to facilitate learning in others, remembering how she stacked reams of paper in the local paper mill for nine years after leaving school. She learned then that inequality breeds strong resentment, and has worked against it ever since. That is her simple explanation for washing the doorstep of her own store. She could not accept anyone else doing what she was not prepared to do when necessary.

Yorkshire Woman of the Year as seen by local artist Tony Heald. *Tony Heald*

Her far-sighted boss in the mill, Eric Orlanda, spotted her potential, gradually mentoring her towards promotion and representing him in different capacities, enabling her to travel for the first time outside the town. These were the days when youth culture was beginning to emerge, when the teenager was invented. With the birth of a generation for whom the war was history, the Beatles helped wipe out a slice of the class system and few intended to emulate their parents. Rita Britton swung into the Sixties too and decided to sell new, fresh and exciting fashions in the old, tired and unexciting town of Barnsley.

On an early buying trip to London she was stunned by one Sloane Ranger's patronising attitude. Slowly she learnt that the woman's entrenched snobbery and arrogance were far more of a permanent handicap than a Barnsley accent was going to be for her. 'I was very naïve, very simplistic', she says, 'daft in fact. I know now what the obstacles were; had I known then I would never have attempted it. I was in the advantageous position of not having good advice or experienced reasoning guiding me, so I never realised how big a job it was going to be. I just thought it would be great to sell some trendy clothes because it was all I knew anything about, all I was interested in, like most young people

THIRTY TWO STEPS, NEAR BARNSLEY

George Porter's family on the Thirty two steps. In the background is the old Paper Mill. *The Goldsborough family collection*

were'. Those were the days when she wore a younger woman's clothes, before she learnt however motivated you are, however laterally you think, there are some barriers that you just cannot break down, because they exist only in the minds of others. Still fired by the urge to have available in, and for, Barnsley what she saw in shops across the south she forgot the rules. 'Do I know your father?' was the puzzling response from a local solicitor when she made an appointment to arrange to buy her own premises for the first time. It was not until years later that she understood the significance of the question.

Falling in love with an accountant was a happy diversion, unplanned but intense. She would have been happy at that stage, and to a great extent would still today, to become the centre of a big and happy family and just be Geoffrey Britton's wife. But despite having two sons and adopting a third, she continued to develop the business interest as her reputation as Pollyanna soared. 'I've never been a planner I'm pulled by tides, I drift with them, I don't have a future in that sense. You might say I don't have a past either'. She doesn't have a single cutting about herself or the store, nor does she actually know where she ends and the store begins. She lives, eats, breathes it and doesn't know whether she became it, or it became her, the chic and the golden egg.

For decades now she has been the one Barnsley woman that everyone has heard of. I once sat in Tokyo Airport waiting for an onward flight and was eagerly joined by a young man who told me I was the only other occidental in the terminal that day. We spoke each other's language for half an hour agreeing we were either almost related or nearly next-door neighbours since he was from Derby and I was from Barnsley. When his flight call took him off an elderly Japanese man sitting nearby stood up smiled, bowed and said, 'Excuse me,?' 'Yes' I replied, then 'Hai' flaunting

Rita Britton photographed by her son John Britton, new member of the Association of Photographers. In this, his first year he has two entries accepted for their prestigious annual awards. *John Britton*

my fluent Japanese. He bowed again, 'Barnsrey?' I smiled agreement not wishing to exhibit my rapidly decreasing verbal skills, as he said, 'Porryanna!' In total disbelief I managed another 'Hai,' as my flight was called leaving no time to find out more. Unable to read the signs, fumbling for my boarding pass and passport with four bags of duty free shopping to gather up, I never-the-less managed a deft, 'arigato' as he helped me with my hand luggage. A final 'sayonara' used up all of my conversational skill and I left, wondering then, and to this day how he knew about Barnsley and Pollyanna.

She has that effect on people. If she were an actor on stage or film, she would be the one that you never looked away from. She is in her own production, re-casting or re-inventing her own personal appearance constantly. She has met just about everyone in the fashion and art world for the last quarter of a century. At Jean Muir's memorial service the shopkeeper from Barnsley was escorted to her named seat in the front pew in St Martin's in the Field. Seated in her named seat, four pews behind her was a woman who had once been Prime Minister of England, but had clearly impressed Jean Muir less than Rita Britton had.

For her too it is not politics or status, so much as integrity, that win her respect. Baroness Denton, a Conservative in the House of Lords became a close friend before her untimely death. Unlike Elizabeth Peacock MP, who lost her job on the principle of opposing pit closures, Jean Denton had not foreseen the policy's potential for the devastation of the local communities being so widespread. As the Baroness ended her first visit to the store in Barnsley, she was given a token gift. It was a copy of the *Book in a Day*, written by the Grimethorpe community. It expressed their feelings about losing the ninety nine year old pit, which had provided a living, for some of them going back five generations, and translated their feelings of pain, anger, resentment, rage, fear, insecurity, sadness, loss and devastation for people who were unaware of them. She accepted the token but said, 'That's a bit below the belt.' 'That's what we thought about the pit closures,' replied Rita Britton, who with Geoff Britton and Nigel McCulloch then Bishop of Wakefield, arrived at seven in the morning to be first to support the project, knowing exactly what it meant. Baroness Denton was then all the more respected by Rita Britton when she subsequently admitted to her, 'I think we got it wrong, we could have done it differently'.

After Jean Denton's death Rita Britton was told by a civil servant who had worked with her, how great an impact the views of that mining community had had on her, and how she regretted not having been aware of the community's feelings. Clearly she had not heard Billy Joel's *Allentown*, or Jimmy Nail singing *Big River*, or any of the wonderful music and lyrics local teacher Dick Walker brought to *Children of the Dark*.

It is most likely that Jean Denton sought her out as a result of the input Rita Britton had made as a member of the National Skills Task Force.

Nigel McCulloch, then Bishop of Wakefield, one of the first supporters to arrive to write the Book in a Day. *Stephen McClarence*

Her maverick style and individual perceptions, whilst frequently too threatening for minnows in small ponds, certainly had an impact on the big fish in the national and international pools of influential policy. Her grass-rooted ability to use her personal experience and observations, in her uniquely anecdotal fashion, made her highly sought after and carefully listened to. She was regarded by many as the open window, providing enough fresh air for artificial respiration as well as oxygen to new-born initiatives.

At local level I contend that her greatest contribution was her work in schools. It is not easy, if you have as high a profile as she has, to work in the shadows, but she has done it. An enabler, a benefactor, a role model, she has worked voluntarily for youngsters for twenty years to my knowledge, as well as serving on several governing bodies of Colleges nationally and locally. It is widely accepted that she was the driving force behind the creation and development of the Design Centre, where she worked tirelessly for years to set up a designer manufacturing base in the town to offer new opportunities for local talent.

It was her personal influence alone that brought Manny Silverman, then highly regarded Adviser to the British Fashion Council, to Barnsley. Not for a visit or two and then back on the 125 from Sheffield, but for six years this Freeman of the Borough of London travelled to the town as Chairman of the Barnsley Design Centre Group. His experience at national board level brought a quality of input to the town that would have been difficult if not impossible, to provide locally. Never once did the man charge even his travelling expenses, paying his own rail fare and eating the sandwiches Rita Britton made for him on the train going home.

Sometimes, being the driving force, means literally driving young hopefuls across the country to meet people in businesses, colleges, newspaper and magazine offices or anywhere else she knows anyone who could help. She accepts every invitation it is physically possible to accept visiting productions, exhibitions and events in schools across the town, and sometimes putting in super-human efforts to do it flying back from New York, Paris or Milan. It is not a glamorous life she leads, it is hard graft in an industry that is as tough as any other.

She is equally keen to support initiatives that are not her own, as she is to suggest and resource those that are. After enjoying school productions she has funded organised theatre visits, including pre-show dinner for the entire cast and back-up team of pupils and staff. Her reward is seeing them discover the buzz of great professional productions, and accepting the prospect and possibility of being a part of it. She uses her contacts to set up opportunities for children to meet, learn from and talk to people like Julia Ormond newly back from filming with Harrison Ford, Sean Connery or Richard Gere, not name-dropping, but sharing the big-time. But it is also time and effort consuming, and the hundreds of individual approaches she receives every year are draining. Now she has a system of challenging young whims and fancies, requiring proof positive of

Rita Britton accepts the Freemanship of Barnsley. *John Britton*

personal intention and enthusiasm, not just a wander round the store and a vague chat, whilst fingering the stock.

She is singularly unpretentious and awed by the rewards of a business that took her over rather than the reverse. She is vulnerable still as a result of her educational experience, and wary of speaking in academic company but does it anyway. She was awarded an honorary doctorate by the University of Hallam. 'I hug it to me,' she says, 'it is incredibly important to me. I sometimes think I will put it on my business cards so I can see it's true every time I give one away. But that would look like bragging, so I don't, though if I ever did brag it would have to be about that, and about getting the Freemanship of the Borough of Barnsley'. She is the first independent woman to be awarded that honour and her acceptance speech in the grand Chamber of the Town Hall was both stirring and funny.

She is in fact wrong, about never bragging. I have heard her, on three separate occasions. The first time was when her eldest son Mark painted two twelve feet high portraits of miners in support of the campaign against pit closures. They were first used as backcloths for the production of *Children of the Dark* at the Civic Hall Barnsley in 1993. Following that they were loaned, for hanging in a local school, to remind the community of the support there had been for the industry. Rodney Bickerstaffe, then General Secretary of Unison, came from London to speak at the unveiling of the twin paintings, which was done simultaneously by the Mayors of Barnsley and Brierley. As TV and newspaper cameras whirred and flashed, I heard Rita Britton's voice say, 'That's my son, he painted those'. The second occasion was when her middle son, computer consultant James used his considerable skill setting up the innovative website for Pollyanna, enabling her to invite her worldwide client base to shop on line. The last time was when John, the youngest, held the first professional exhibition of his work as a photographer, and virtually sold out.

Mark Britton's work on stage at Barnsley Civic Hall for the production of *Children of the Dark*, 1993. *The author*

She concedes the recollections, 'I know, I never really had any ambition until I had my sons, I wanted them to grow up with fewer constraints than I had. I wanted most of all for them to be fair-minded liberal thinkers, but hard working too, because that is bred in them just like it is in me from my Dad and my Grandma. When I ask if, and when, she set out to be a rebel, she instinctively rejects the idea. A second of reflection brings a review and she agrees that she must look like one though it was always unintentional. 'I suppose I was a bit of a Dyno-Rod in my day; but I only deal with seriously blocked drains now.' She is aware that the closer to the fire, the more you get burned, but can't keep out of the kitchen. If you do nothing, there is very little you can or will be blamed for, but she can't live with it. Just as she persuades me that she has already achieved more then she ever thought of, let alone aspired to, I feel the wind change. 'Do you know,' she thinks aloud, 'somebody ought to do something about getting this town a theatre big enough for big stars to want to come, and where everyone could easily learn to love music, drama, theatre in every form. I ask her if that is her new dream. 'No' she says instantly, 'My dream is grandkids who will think I'm cool or fantastic or rebellious. I won't wear purple when I'm old, but I might have a tattoo just so nobody can tell me I'll regret it when I'm older'.

Former captain of British Lions Rugby League Team, and member of 1972 World Championship squad. David Topliss is a regular supporter of the Lamproom Theatre. Here with the cast of Chris Evans' production of *Up and Under* by John Godber from the left Barry Askam, Dave Topliss, Richard Caile, Pete Foster, Paul Haley, Phil Shepherd, Chris Evans and Louise Armitage. *The author*

She has a rare gift, the ability to take genuine pleasure in the achievements of others. She is over the moon when she hears local hairdresser Robert Eaton has won yet another trophy, to add to his collection, and breaks off to run to the salon to congratulate him. Her role models are unstoppable, diverse, creative and kind and, not in the business in which she has made her own name. Her ability for sheer hard graft was both learnt from and genetically gifted by her grandmother who she tries to emulate. She finds Sir Ernest Hall and his creation of the arts centre, Dean Clough in Halifax, truly inspirational. 'He is so multi talented. There seems to be nothing that daunts him,' she says. 'Can you imagine he became a concert pianist in his forties, and in his fifties he took up horse riding. There are no fences in life that he can't jump. I just hope I'm around to see what he does in his eighties'.

Equally highly she rates Jonathan Silver who before his tragically early death had been a close friend. His creation of the Salts Mill complex shines out, like a Turner sky in his memory. It is the one place in the

Cast Members of the Lamproom Theatre, Barnsley, with the author of 'Up n Under', John Godber, when he visited the theatre to see the production. Amateur or semi-professional actors, they were thrilled to receive his support. Even greater celebration followed when the production won two major prizes. Out of hundreds of entries nation-wide, they won Best Production Award in the National Drama Festival's Association All-Winners Festival in July 2003. To achieve this success they beat 71 other short-listed entries for the title of Best Amateur Theatre in the country. The production also won the award for Backstage Technical Performance. *The author*

world and he was the one man who could have drawn David Hockney back to show and share his talent in the area. Even greater than her own immense sadness, she feels the loss for his wife and daughters, sharing their grief and anger that he died when he had so much left to give and to achieve.

Despite being paired with Dickie Bird for the town's highest honours she is not a cricket fan. Her choice of a sportsman, is based on criteria other than sporting prowess. 'Geoffrey Boycott is one of the most thoughtful and kindest men I know' she reveals. Following her battle with breast cancer twenty years ago, she remembers, and always will, Boycott's friendship, concern and generous offers of support to cheer her through bleak days.

Author John Godber who wrote one of his earliest works, Blockages, during the degree course he completed at Bretton Hall College in the 1970s. He spent the summer working 'on the bins' in Barnsley. *The author*

She plays down achieving the improbable, but it is indisputable that she has enhanced the image and perception of Barnsley, far and wide, and inspired a new generation of Barnsley's best to go out and do the same. When I ask her what's next, she is serious, 'Why don't we start a campaign to get Ken Dodd on at *The Lamproom*?'

21
Ronnie Dukes and Ricki Lee

Stage Performers

One of the first youngsters to consult Rita Britton was a student at Derby College of Art. Nervously but successfully showing her designs in Pollyanna she was not only encouraged, but commissioned to design and make garments for the store. They both remember still how Susan Woolf once spent a Christmas Eve sewing tiny buttons onto an outfit for a client whilst Rita Britton, then a young mother with a child balanced on one hip, dashed round three times to see if the creation was ready for Ricki Lee to wear that night.

These were the days when the entertainment capital of the country was not in the south, but squarely set in Yorkshire. *Batley Variety Club* brought the biggest names in the world to perform for local audiences. A young Paul Daniels moved from the North East to live in a caravan in Cawthorne, Barnsley to be in the hub of things, geographically located for easy access to the venues. Mining was a thriving industry, and now paying its workers well. The spin-off in terms of business, commerce and leisure was unprecedented.

Barnsley, Wakefield, Sheffield, Chesterfield were spokes on a dazzling wheel of talent and stardom, that spun magic and circles of celebrity into the hard playing ends of hard working days. Eartha Kitt vied with Shirley Bassey, Dave Allen with Allen King, Morecambe and Wise with The Three Degrees, Tony Christie with Jack Jones, Cannon and Ball with The Grumbleweeds, Tommy Cooper with Freddie Starr. In varying degrees, they all won the appreciation of the increasingly discerning local audiences. Sell-outs were routine, but despite the world class appearances, the hottest ticket in town was always, Dukes and Lee.

Small, round and comically lethal, Ronnie Dukes headed a family of such talent that it swept them from early days of pubs and working men's clubs to the Royal Variety Command Performance and *This is your Life*. His potentially anarchic sharp and critically Jewish presentation contrasted incongruously with his stunning wife, gentler, tall, blonde, Kim Bassinger look-a-like style and with a terrific singing voice. He would stand behind her as she reduced the audience to total silence with *My Yiddish Mama*, seriously indicating in mime that her teeth were false. Her mother, playing piano accompaniment, would silently admonish him with a glare so intense that he would reel backwards then bounce back bringing chaos to the number. Ricki Lee would patiently outstand him

Dukes and Lee live on stage. *The Dukes' family collection*

and pull it all back together with a final verse or chorus. The audience, no matter how often they had seen the routine, would be euphoric.

They worked hard and played hard, essentially a family unit, their hospitality was legendary, and their three children Dean, Perry and Jolie regularly met showbiz legends, on and off stage. Perry remembers trying out new football strips brought back from the North East for him and brother Dean. Playing in the garden they were unexpectedly joined by Freddie Starr, who having no strip, stripped down to his underpants to play in goal. Ricki's intervention was a failed attempt to save the neighbours' blushes. 'Freddie you can't play dressed like that!' brought an apparently sincere apology from Starr, followed by chaos as the anarchic comic removed his underpants.

The couple's young daughter, Jolie, was too young, but Dean and Perry were both members of the stage act, which also included Ray Wafer (guitar) Pete Parkinson (sax) Pete Middleton (trumpet) Terry Herrington (keyboards).

Ronnie Dukes' drumming, dancing, singing, satirically comedic and acrobatically pratt-falling skills were legendary. For years he refused television offers on the basis that he could use, and polish to perfection, the same material for months in the clubs. Every TV appearance would entail new material, all of which he wrote himself. Word of mouth however, can prove as fast a spur as fame, and reluctantly the family were drawn into stressful and faster paced, bigger exposure than they wanted. Ronnie Dukes died back stage in Jersey in 1981 and his young widow died tragically early in 1986. The boys never quite found the heart to continue with that degree of pressure, without their parents, at the same level.

But they have memories that are rare, even in the world of show business. Following their appearance on The Royal Command Performance they were presented to the Queen and Prince Philip. The tall, elegant Prince looked down at Ronnie and commented, 'Good Lord, you're very small for a dancer.' The comic looked up at him and came back, 'With all respect Sir I used to be taller. I was as tall as you before I started dancing.' Her Majesty was amused, and like every other fan the duo met, asked the same question, 'Is the lady who plays the piano really your mother-in-law?' She received exactly the same reply as every other fan, 'I wouldn't have her in the act if she wasn't would I, Ma'am?' Happy days and a sad sad loss when these brilliant performers died so young.

Lord Delfont presents Ricki Lee and Ronnie Dukes to Her Majesty The Queen. *The Dukes' family collection*

22

Susan Wolff

Designer, Consultant, Property Developer

On completion of her degree at Derby College of Art Susan Wolff was given a one-year contract in the design room of a local company. S R Gent's major client was Marks and Spencer, at that time on a mission to take themselves out of the double-gusseted, twin-setted, middle-aged market for which they had famously catered. Designing night-dresses for Marks and Spencer was not the stuff of her dreams after satisfying design work at Pollyanna and the interaction of College, but it was a start, and an opportunity to see business transacted at local level. The end of the year coincided with Marks and Spencer expanding their business with S R Gent, and she was asked to design blouses, then dresses, and eventually the entire women's range.

Success brought promotion, wider responsibilities and extensive travel, with frequent visits to London seeing and feeling the excitement of being in a vital industry. It was exciting, different and motivating and for a while Barnsley was left behind, as she learned 'you have to be on the spot to be on the ball, to be sure of winning at anything.'

She knew instinctively that she was capable of competing in this new world and producing results. The work was hard, but she thrived on it, always using the Barnsley yardstick for effort which came naturally to her. Her talent, hard work and personality caught the eye of S R Gent's chairman, they were eventually married, and she felt she had to work even harder. I suggest she is simply a compulsive worker, but had not yet either realised or accepted the fact. Her feeling is, 'That's probably right, the person I am had no choice actually. I have always felt I wanted to work, even though I was financially secure'.

It seems she is of the same breed as Rita Britton in this regard. Such multi-talented and multi-task capable women, are allowed no quarter in the cut-throat world they inhabit. Logic abounds to mitigate their achievements, and beauty is often a distinct liability. In this high-flying world, Susan Wolff found that one of the loneliest places to be was sitting on the Board of Directors of an international company, as the only woman. After ten years in fashion she felt she was in a rut. Analytically sifting through her achievements and what she had still to achieve, she concluded that she no longer felt passionate about designing. Black or blue, short or long, she didn't really care any more, so it was time to stop. Her explanation, 'Designing is a young game,' is frightening when you realise that she was just thirty years old.

One of her strengths is that she never allows herself the luxury of deciding what she does not want to do, before she rationalises and identifies what she does want to do. She felt a need for innovative ideas, envisaging a new team of designers with different techniques and designs, introducing hand-stitching on clothing made overseas, with the highly skilled Barnsley staff undertaking the training of new staff and controlling quality. Her previous achievements ensured management's confidence in her ability and she was appointed Managing Director of S R Gent's International Division. The job brought work and stress levels which would have broken many, but equally high levels of excitement and satisfaction. Within a year she had exceeded all expectations, and found herself in charge of a team of designers and production staff, responsible for total management of the import element. This was no doubt a contributing factor when the University of Leeds awarded her a Fellowship for services to the fashion industry.

Looking back, some twenty years later, she recalls the risk-taking and responsibility as frightening but identifies it as 'the most electrifying buzz of my professional life'. If the trips from Barnsley to London had looked significant back in the early days of her career, they paled in comparison with the international travel that now became her routine. Personal involvement was crucial, at every level which meant organising her work, her life and her family to be free to make trips to China, the Philippines and Sri Lanka on a regular basis.

There are two perspectives of such a life style. Those who do not live at that level, see sheer privilege. Jet-setting, wining and dining, entertaining, power-dressing and freedom to spend one's considerable earnings in the best outlets in the world. Those who live it often see a different picture. Hours or days of waiting at airports, being stuck in traffic in foreign countries driving a car on the wrong side of the road, always eating in restaurants, smiling until your face hurts at people with whom you have nothing in common but work, having to eat the fish eye because it is the tradition and you are the honoured guest, even though you are jet-lagged or pregnant, or both, not to mention missing one's own home and family.

By 1990 Susan Wolff had a son and daughter of her own, and had also fostered two little girls. She recalls that travel was so much a routine in their young lives that once on a trip from London to Brighton the children thought they would need foreign currency to buy an ice cream. This dual life style was possible because of her own organisation and capacity for work, but also because of the tremendous support she has always had from her family. She insists she could not have functioned as a wife, mother and managing director without their backing.

After seven years, she wondered if the buzz, the widening of her horizons and the tremendous feeling of success were really worth the price she was paying. Her own health, quality of life, relationships and the speed with which she saw the children growing up, became the new priority and challenge. Sitting in Shanghai Airport after missing a plane she found herself repeatedly putting the same question to herself, 'Why am I doing this?' She spent the time drawing up two lists, reasons to be there, and reasons not to be there. Seeing how much longer the second list was, on her return to London she gave a year's notice of her intention to give up the job. In six years, with her team, she had transformed an operation with no turnover into one with a turnover of forty million pounds, constituting forty per cent of the entire business of the organisation. It had been exhilarating, the achievement enormously satisfying but weighing the balance, she decided, enough was enough.

What she did next may be what she is generally best known for, the Susan Wolff line of women's clothing. Blazoned above twenty-four boutiques around the UK and the continent, her name together with the gentle, natural fabrics in sleekly cut designs that ranged from the sharply professional, to the elegantly casual and the subtly sexy were a magnet. Understated chic in muted shades whispered taste and distinction, transforming power dressing into an art form of femininity. They became fashion 'had to haves' of the 1990s.

Designing and setting the tone again, she felt a wave of satisfaction, but it was tempered by other factors. The business was on a far smaller scale than she was accustomed to, despite the quality and geographical breadth of the outlets. The creative side was out weighed by the other tasks, funding locations for stores PR and retail training of staff. Feeling she would not match her previous achievements she gave up her post. Not being part of the core development that S R Gent needed to concentrate on at a difficult time in its history, the Susan Wolff business was sold.

Now, she thought, she should concentrate on the full-time running of a house and home, and being a Mum. After three months of total commitment to the role she was a little taken aback to be asked by her eldest child if she had considered going back to work. She had not at that point, but the following week out of the blue was offered the position of Marketing Director for Asprey, the London jewellers. The offer was flattering, re-assuring, even challenging. It was a prestigious company, a luxury product, a new and interesting direction and it represented a technical challenge, which grew more inviting every time she thought about it. Encouraged by her family, the next time the offer was made, she accepted.

She looks back on it now as one of the best decisions she ever made, personally or professionally. A completely new world opened up and she quickly adapted to meet the range and challenge of the new career, on her travels identifying sources and manufacturers worldwide. Her eye for cut and colour was now widened to include clarity and carat as she

Susan Wolff. *Susan Wolff's collection*

sought and bought the most beautiful gemstones in the world, for some of the most discerning customers. She took the decisions on what designs would be created for display in some of the most exclusive show cases, and designed some of the most expensive pieces in the world. Private commissions for personal jewellery, from families such as that of the Sultan of Brunei, became a routine part of her day and she loved it all. Under Susan Wolff's guidance and fed by her enthusiasm, Asprey saw its sales increase dramatically and an Asprey ring now became the engagement symbol of the nineties. Designing jewellery for such a top-class firm meant that the evidence of her craft would be permanent, achievement literally set in stones.

Susan Wolff, like Rita Britton, understands the need to mix the day's range with the line, cut and style of classic basics for a complete wardrobe, of complete women. Her lasting hero, is Georgio Armani. 'The cut is superb and his eye for colour is unbelievable, he is in a class of his own. In twenty years I have never seen anyone to touch him'.

She defines talent as the natural ability to sing, dance or paint well, not accepting her own versatility. Attractive and articulate, with a soft voice that belies her sense of purpose and intent, she says her strengths are organisation, and an ability to learn from listening. She is right, but I would add her ability to use those skills to achieve her own potential and that of others working with her. Equally important is her ability to re-invent herself in changing situations. When I tell her she can have only one word to describe herself, she chooses grafter. 'You have to give up part of your life to get the equal reward for what you are prepared to put in,' she says, 'I have worked for every bit of success I've had, but I've been lucky enough to get it'.

She never forgets her roots and how important they are, and is living proof that you can take the girl out of Barnsley but not Barnsley out of the girl. 'Barnsley is my slippers, I love coming home' I ask her who designed the slippers and what design they are. 'I did of course, and they are very cosy, very relaxing, very Barnsley. They are as comfortable as the people here, but they do have a bit of jewellery on the front, encrustment, sparkling, Asprey style, I think.'

She is youthful, beautiful, female and strong, and has managed a life of a warm home, three generations of family unity, balanced with international careers of enormous variety, all with panache and success. Skiing, sunning and dividing herself between home, work and play, in homes in Switzerland and Knightsbridge, have been compensations for the abject hard work. Pacing her life to a more relaxed mode, she is now fulfilled, and involved in a new venture rather than compelled by it. Happy marriage to equally successful American dish Marc Winer, includes partnership in yet another direction, property development, bringing her back to Barnsley, which she still calls home. As we veer off course into less serious vein she tells me about the amazing new hair products recommended to her by the staff in Liberty's, and wonders if she might be able to buy them elsewhere. Happily I am able to tell her she can get them at *REAL hairdressing*, Cale Street Chelsea where a lad from Barnsley has got a salon.

Susan Wolff has lived a life that Alice Robinson used to sit in cinemas and dream about. She has never stopped working, exudes ultimate class and is all woman. And she remains the girl I knew more than thirty years ago.

23
Romilly Mullen

Designer

Not yet in the Asprey and Garrard league but rising fast is Romilly Mullen, recently appointed to design jewellery for the Kenneth Cole range in the Liz Claiborne organisation. Living most of her life in Ackworth, but unlike her brother Matthew and sister Martha, born in Barnsley, where her father, Terry Mullen, has spent his life teaching mathematics. Currently Assistant Head of Penistone Grammar School, he approves the school's links to Nicholas Saunderson, eminent mathematician, and regarded as one of the most distinguished men this country ever produced. Born in 1682, blinded by smallpox in infancy, Saunderson never-the-less went on to teach at Cambridge. A Fellow of the Royal Society in 1711 and elected professor of Mathematics 1727 his highly esteemed work, *Algebra* and other mathematical writings were printed posthumously in 1740.

Mullen himself chairs the Mathematics Subject Advisory Committee for the Assessment and Qualification Alliance, now the largest examination board in the UK. A fascinating maths teacher he once began an assessment lecture to a group of art students with a poem *The Beauty of Mathematics* produced after one of his lessons by a fourteen year old pupil. Now that is teaching, done by the best headteacher Barnsley never had.

Terry Mullen arrives at Bretton Hall as guest lecturer. *The author*

His own youngest daughter, Romilly, developed her learning with an interestingly wide selection of subject to study for 'A' levels, politics, psychology and art. It became clear which specialism she preferred in her next move, to Clarendon College in Nottingham, where she did a Foundation Course in Art and Design. The core components offered an equally wide choice for further up-take, with resistant materials metal, glass and ceramics, combined with constructed textiles, life drawing and finally photography.

By now she was clear what direction she wanted to take, the design and manufacture of jewellery. The technical theory was essential for industry and craft applications but it was the creative element that fascinated her. Her final year at Nottingham Trent, brought her the BA Honours, in Textile Design that she wanted, but an unexpected bonus, which proved a great kick start in the business she had decided was to be hers. Her final exhibition collection of jewellery was bought by Millie of London.

For many students, the hard slog for a decent degree and a final exhibition would justify a long rest and an easy summer. The local work ethic does not support that however, and particularly not when you belong to a family who believe in 'grafting': that is actually earning the money you receive for work done, not merely hold a position for which you are paid. Being of such a breed made the summer question simple. She needed a break, but she also needed time to assess the situation to research the market into which she hoped to break.

As a freelance, she took consultancy work in a London fashion store at the high end of the market. She was responsible for all the visual merchandising of the store, from window displays to the total co-ordination of both men and women's fashion departments. This created a view for others to see and be drawn by her work but also widened her own perspectives. The more focussed observation, and requirement for attention to every minute detail, sharpened her vision. Time spent researching at university was helpful now, in that she had been given time and space to see the wide world of merchandising and design, to observe, know and be influenced by it. She had total responsibility for every aspect in a clearly defined small piece of a larger mosaic.

The Chaos Theory, that a butterfly flaps its wings in Kansas and causes a storm in Brazil, is perhaps also possible as a creative theory. Her detailed co-ordination of the many designers in stock for both men and women required her to ensure simultaneously that fluency in the style and ethos of the whole store was maintained. This was invaluable and new insight into the world of practical merchandising, and the philosophy A level came into play.

With this sharper perception she could identify market trends as well as fashion lines. Her view was that the consumer climate matched the slightly depressed financial trend, and that accessories now were a dominant and multi-functional feature. They were the means of simply and relatively inexpensively transforming last season's garment into this season's look, and were financially suited to impulse and pocket. For another market niche they were a reward, a must-have, a keep-up with the trendy-spenders. She set about designing her own innovative, contemporary jewellery, and was spot on target in both marketing and creativity as her sales throughout the UK verified.

She was also on the move. Within a year she was in New York working for American Eagle Outfitters. Again the brief was widened, but so were the opportunities to learn. Her responsibilities included researching of trends, so formalising what she had already done for herself previously. She then had to devise colour and design concepts for jewellery and hair accessories, as younger and younger children followed the pied pipers and ranks of teenagers into the hair braiding revolution, so the demand for accessories and ornamental jewellery to customise themselves grew. So too did Romilly Mullen's design packages, increasing to accommodate or inspire them. The company was not large enough for separate departments in technical, purchasing co-ordination, sales, marketing and production matters. Rather than being put off by this, she readily welcomed it as an opportunity to expand her experience and with it her potential for promotion.

She enjoyed contact with overseas and domestic buyers as much as the creative side of the business. Long legged, blonde, beautiful and personable she had enough eye appeal to make her promotional presentations attractive, but that would not stand the acid test of selling and buying. Her designs and merchandising experience led to increased sales and her emerging acumen increased her status and reputation, in the industry.

With a young foot on a big ladder, she has an apartment in Brooklyn Heights with a sky-line view of New York, leads the life that goes with it, and loves it. Frequently home, as her extended family grows with the births of nephews and niece Jake, Asha and Noah, one thing about her is as clear as crystal. You can be half-way round the world but if you are part of a family as strong as Jane and Terry Mullen have created, you never forget who or what you are, however high the heights.

24

Josh Wood

Hairdresser

He never considered going down the pit, he wanted to be a hairdresser. He got himself on a YTS scheme and thought he was on his way. A year later they finished him, advising him to find a different job, since he would not make a hairdresser. He found a different salon, and another, finally deciding it was too traditional for him, he could not fit the moulds that were everywhere. Even a move to Leeds and a more corporate style with Vidal Sassoon, left him feeling his personality was still leashed. He moved to London's Sloane Street and life of a new order but still could not settle. He was nineteen, missed his friends and family in the North and had no cash. Back North with Vidal Sasoon he spent half his time in Leeds and half in Manchester for a year and found it exhausting. He was succeeding but not living.

Vacancies in South Moulton Street opened London for him again, but this time on his terms. He had learned the ropes and got a better deal, including an apartment, and in return was happy to work the ten to twelve hour days. He was earning serious money and, by twenty one, had a serious reputation as an Assisting Session Hairdresser. The cover of *Vogue*, working with top designers Rifat Ozbeck, Azzardine Alliah jetting to Japan, Europe, New York or LA, he became highly sought after. He was adaptable and as good at assisting as taking charge. The research side of the business began to interest him as much as the creative, as he was involved developing product content for Proctor and Gamble.

By now he was really in the big time. Fashion show work led on to other contracts as he became the fashion himself. Stars like Bowie, Jagger, and Minogue trusted their hair to him, the mega wealthy would fly him anywhere in the world to be there for their next big occasion. He is still rooted firmly himself, and laughs at being the only passenger on a 747 to New York, sent to bring him for one special client, on his own with a bedroom on a plane! He doesn't say who, it's the discretion, the confidentiality that keeps him in there as much as his undisputed talent as a colourist. He feels able to name those who have no objection to being named, but their conversations are not for discussion with anyone.

By the age of twenty three his work for Vidal Sassoon took him to New York. Thought by some to be too dangerous, he loved the place, and the American concept that how good you are is all that matters. In London there was still the notion that who you were mattered as much. It never

Josh Wood and Belle Cannan demonstrate their REAL polish and perfect condition. *Chalk PR*

had to him, and still didn't. Who he was, incidentally, was the hairdresser who was in demand to go on their world tours with famous artistes. It was unreal to someone as unpretentious as he is. He felt unable to accept success of that order and would be at the biggest celebrity parties and find himself wanting to take the canapés or drinks round.

He bought a property in Brixton and moved back to the UK. As Director of Colour for Sassoon it was still the high life, lunch at Windsor Castle, parties at Kensington Palace, but hard work in big demand meant working fifteen to sixteen hours a day.

He had met Belle Cannan when they trained together in the early years before she left Vidal Sassoon to start Nicky Clarke's salon in Mount Street, becoming his top stylist. They now dovetail perfectly in their own new salon in Chelsea, so successfully they have had to expand. Their latest development is the launch of their own range of products for hair care. Personal diagnosis and customised shampooing, conditioning vitamin and mineral treatments, using the products found by Susan Wolff on sale in Liberty, attracts their target clientele. It is pampering without a doubt, but they both exude more warmth and common sense than exclusivity.

They have a meeting before the salon opens, which follows mine with Josh at 7.45 am, it is the only time in three days he is free for half and hour. I have never met him before but I get the free spot to talk to him about his success.

He is relaxed, friendly, shrewd and on the ball, an experienced, travelled, connected, cooperative, funny, unspoilt belter of a kid from Barnsley. He loves to 'come home', his best friends are still here and he is delighted to see a gradual development of culture, and more expansive leisure entertainment in the town. Admittedly drifting in his earlier years, he would now consider opening a salon in the emerging renaissance of the town. He can do what he wants to do, only goes where he's comfortable and loves his life. 'I never went after all this you know, I didn't know it was there. Standing up to eighteen hours a day I sometimes say I would have been better off going down a pit' he laughs 'I might have had beat knees but these varicose veins aren't glamorous either'. Maybe not, but they could be what you get when your feet are so firmly on the ground.

25
Calendar Girls

Charity Fundraisers

Given the chance, you really should not miss them – The Calendar Girls, or Baker's Half Dozen, as they now are known. A great after dinner performance of rib-aching, mascara streaking mischief and self-deprecation in aid of Leukaemia and Lymphoma Research. Two of the six readily identify themselves as Barnsley girls, with links that they feel as strongly today as ever. Describing themselves as nobodies, they might just be the most photographed nobodies in the world since posing for 'that calendar'.

Coast to Coast personal appearances on American TV's highest rated chat shows predictably followed their overnight success in the UK. The

Bakers Half Dozen, from the left Lynda Logan, Beryl Bamforth, Tricia Stewart, Christine Clancy, Angela Baker and Ros Fawcett. *Terry Logan*

full account of how the calendar came about is candidly recorded in Tricia Stewart's warm and eminently readable book *Calendar Girl*. The account gives a comprehensive insight into the personalities of the girls, including our two from Barnsley.

When Prince Charles, allegedly, identified Lynda Logan as his personal favourite it gave her the ultimate vehicle to perfect her self-confessed penchant for posing. It's a Barnsley thing, candour of that order. Her signature on the collectable new photograph of Baker's Half Dozen, wickedly flaunts the patronage, triumphantly declares superior status and puts a glint of gloating in her eye. It is slow-timing at the highest level. She is, she knows well, a member of a team that is nothing if it is not a team, each member of it dependant on the others whilst giving the same degree of support to them. Mutual respect and affection has enabled this small, now much copied, group of women to aim realistically to raise a million pounds, all for the Leukaemia Research Fund. Along the way they have inspired the making of a film about them which has, with only one or two notable omissions, starring in it the very best of British actresses today.

Originality, sauciness, incongruity, humour, and good taste are the obvious crucial elements in the calendar's success, but undoubtedly the most important additional ingredient is the sheer quality of the photography. Lynda's husband, Terry Logan, had the imagination, eye for detail, creativity and sheer artistic talent together with a lifetime of photographic experience, and a position of trust within the group, that transformed what started as a joke into a reality. The perfect backcloth for the scenes was agreed to be the Logan's wonderful old house in the Dales. The house was built in 1642 by a Francis Hewitt and the couple, especially Lynda, had felt an immediate and unaccountable sense of coming home from the minute they walked through the door for the first time. Stranger than fiction, they recently discovered old papers of the builder Francis, and his two brothers Matthew and John Hewitt. One of the wills indicated that in addition to the land that the Logan's now owned, the family also owned land in Darton, Barnsley, where Lynda was born.

Lynda Morris left Keighley Technical School to work in a local wool mill, in the leaflet-mailing department. Sketching models and then modelling the samples, led to a

Lynda and Terry Logan at home.
The author

move to the publicity and publishing department of another local factory, where she found herself mastering catalogue lay-outs, working with her new colleague, Terry Logan. The rest, as they say, is history.

Having completed night school training at Bradford Art College both felt that they were increasingly able to combine their technical skills in processing film, with talents of a more artistically creative nature. Despite this, and the fact that the working partnership had blossomed into romance they were unsettled, and felt the need for greater challenge. This time of treading-water professionally, was to prove extremely useful in the distant future, as Terry began honing his skills in portrait photography with Lynda as model, or poseur as she prefers to call it.

The predictable development of marriage came and with it a move to start a new life in Canada. As Art Director for the biggest advertising agency in the world, J Walter Thompson, Terry continued to polish skills that were to become so important nearly thirty years later. Settled and happy, their lives seemed to be completed by the births in 1966 and 1969 of Simon and Georgina. Terry's increasing recognition and success led to them being given a holiday, by the Company, back in the UK. With new eyes they looked again at the North of England and Lynda decided that for her Canada had no nitty-gritty, it was an egg without a yoke. That pre-requisite for her was where it had always been, in Yorkshire, and they agreed it was time to come back. The high life in Canada was to be exchanged for a good life at home where Terry would paint as he had always wanted to do, so would Lynda. He would see more of the family, and she would work in her aunt's wool shop in Skipton. The window had space for display, and Terry quickly sold the first painting for £20.

Then came a gallery in Gargrave, the front cover of the *Dalesman*, and another success story was beginning. By the 1980s daughter Georgina, with a History of Arts degree was involved in the family business specialising in paintings in silks, and Lynda's increasing involvement led to the need for larger premises, and ultimately to the *Logan Gallery* in Grassington, and a house in Cracoe next door to a family called Baker.

A firm believer in fate as a positive generator of both purpose and outcome in life, Lynda Logan believes it was all meant to be, just as they were meant to live in a house with historic links to Darton. She and Terry were meant to become firm friends with Angela and John Baker, their new neighbours, and Matthew Baker the son, was meant to fall in love with the girl next door, Georgina Logan. Barnsley roots bonded the two women and an instant friendship was formed, with a closeness that would become crucial for all in less than three years, with John Baker's tragically early death.

Together with friends and neighbours in the close-knit, caring community the Logans responded when John Baker was diagnosed as having non-Hodgkin's Lymphoma. Visiting and cheering-up were as difficult as anyone who has lived through similar circumstances will know. The women, all WI members were discussing the annual chore of finding interesting photographs for the WI calendar. Inspirationless they jokingly approved Tricia Stewart's outrageous suggestion of doing all the usual poses of flower-arranging, jam-making, piano-playing which epitomised the WI and its membership – but doing it in the buff. It caused wine-assisted giggling, and did much to raise spirits and the idea became a running joke. John Baker was to be the formal observer, his reward for getting well, and naturally Terry Logan was to be the photographer. Tricia Stewart had a year earlier suggested that Lynda Logan use her artistic talents to paint the group of girlfriends as discreetly covered nudes to serve as a permanent reminder of their youthfulness, in anticipation of lines and droops slowly developing, but it had never taken off as a serious proposition. No one is clear at exactly what point the calendar stopped being a joke and became a perfectly reasonable possibility, but it did. It also became acceptable to enough volunteers, to make it achievable as a practical project, though John Baker laughed and said it would never happen.

The Logans were moving home when John Baker died. It was as if the house had been built for the very purpose it was now to offer, as scenery for the alternative calendar. What had begun as a joke and become a possibility was now a mission. It seemed to them all that they could perhaps offset some of the pain of John's death by making good come out of it. Aside from the support of family and friends needed by all in the face of death, Angela Baker was persuaded that there could be a positive outcome of her struggle to accept what felt like the end of her own reason for living. Tricia Stewart recalls that it happened because of Lynda Logan's pragmatism in galvanising the group into action a week after John's death, as a way of keeping Angela on target.

They could never in their wildest dreams have predicted what followed. Local, regional, and then national media received the story warmly, everyone loved it. Then inter-continental interviews, TV chat shows, personal appearances, they suddenly found they had celebrity status. Whilst their lives changed sensationally and irrevocably, the six who persevered in the original concept of the fund-raising seem amazingly unchanged. They are thrilled, flattered but totally unfazed by the latest development – a blockbuster film about them. They cannot believe that actresses of such calibre as Annette Crosbie, Celia Imrie, Geraldine James and Linda Bissett want to be a part of their story, but find themselves filming alongside them during the day, and discussing characterisation over a meal or bottle of wine in the evenings. Everybody they ever knew has a part in the filming as an extra, and it is an amazing experience to observe the sheer professionalism of the stars in action. We stand and watch Helen Mirren, Julie Walters and Penelope Wilton take and re-take a scene in a marquee at a country fair. It is unbelievable the finesse with which they

Celia Imrie arrives on set to join Annette Crosbie for their scene. *The author*

Geraldine James (with other cast members) had happy memories of filming in Barnsley in 2002. *The author*

Dame Helen Mirren and Lynda Logan on location for the filming of the story of the *Calendar Girls*. *The author*

Helen Mirren and Julie Walters sign some of the hundreds of autographs for fans. *The author*

Penelope Wilton leaves the set after completing her scenes for the day. Voice coach Andrew Jack is in the background, extreme right. *The author*

The real Calendar Girls are rehearsed for their parts as rival W.I. members in the film. *The author*

Linda Bisset and Annette Crosbie with Angela Baker, Beryl Bamforth and Christine Clancey. *The author*

reconstruct exactly the angle, the height, the emotion with such effortless precision again and again and again. Eyebrows arched with mathematical accuracy, shoulders squared with balletic practice, eyes conveying overt intention whilst simultaneously concealing years of training and experience. In contrast, the real Calendar girls demonstrate their ultimate quality of excelling, by being themselves. Beryl January, Angela February, Lynda July, Christine September, Tricia October and Ros November now appear fully clothed as rival WI members in the scene. It is a joy to observe the amateurs and professionals blend with total harmony.

My continuing meetings with the six re-inforces the first impression, they are a uniquely natural combination unfettered by pretension. Thrown unintentionally into a limelight, the intensity of which can accelerate the growth of envy in others, they emerge unchanged. Having weathered the storms that they already have survived collectively and individually, I have every confidence in their ability to survive it all.

Lynda Logan's first lesson in survival came at the age of three, when her father, George Morris, was killed in a traffic accident whilst working as an electrical engineer in Barnsley. It is now thought that he died as a result of suffering a black-out. His post-mortem indicated that he was suffering from leukaemia – Lynda's family's first encounter with the condition. Emma, his widow was left to bring up their children alone. Derek and Enid had died in childhood, each tragedy binding closer the remaining three, Christine, Arthur and Lynda. In keeping with the system of few, if any benefits, Emma Morris understood that it was now her sole responsibility to provide for the material needs of the family whilst attempting to create as happy a childhood for them as it was possible to do. For Lynda Morris it was a magical childhood.

She remembers no complaining as her mother routinely worked full-time and then did the cooking, washing, cleaning and growing vegetables in the garden of 11 Bence Lane, Darton. In her spare time she would knit pullovers for Arthur, and for Christine and Lynda she produced matching cardigans with the then fashionable bobbles on the front. So to Reverend Peverill at Darton Church where Emma also played the organ, Lynda was known as 'Pom Pom'. Emma also managed to keep a social element in her life by joining the successful and popular Darton Dramatic Society.

Lynda Logan and her sister Christine Clarke remember their happy days in Darton with the author. *The author's collection*

Christine would hurry home from Darton Junior School to help in looking after Lynda, forging a bond that remains as touchingly strong today as it was then. They re-live the happy, halcyon Darton days for me in breaks between filming on the set in Burnsall. The scene is the local show and alongside the famous faces are those of virtually the whole families and friends of the Baker's Half Dozen added to enough members of Women's Institutes to provide jam for the entire UK consumption for the next fifty years.

Half a day is spent on a fleeting background shot of the best Dog Competition at the show, and not without incident. Christine plays one of a circle of proud dog owners parading their dogs before the judges. Sky, the Logan's own dog is included and thinks she is Lassie, but from time to time totally disrupts the take, ably assisted by some twenty other dogs. The arrival of Matthew and Georgina Baker with their daughter Helena and four day old new baby Kristina sends Sky into an uncontrollable frenzy of recognition.

Cries of 'Heel' and 'Sit' go unheeded, lost in canine chaos. Christine's husband Stuart, playing one of the judges has no success in attempting to assert his authority, despite being assisted by the twenty other dog handlers, and a lot of advice from the watching crowd. The Logan's son Simon, with wife Emma and grandson Edward give the performance of the day, pretending that they are strangers to the area, and have never seen the disruptive animal before in their lives. They are joined in this by the Baker's daughter Rachel, her husband Neil and their children Emma and Harry. It is a joyous farce to observe and I wonder silently if it was wise to include a dog show in the hectic two day shoot which already has several competitions, a fair, Morris Dancers, and children in fancy dress. Order is finally restored and when everyone has fussed over the new baby and canine sanity is regained, we return to reminiscing. What they all dream of is a world and a future as happy and safe as theirs had been for these little ones. Days long-gone when children could play happily on Rabbit Hill behind Bence Lane until the disappearing sun had mothers standing on doorsteps calling them in. The only wistfulness, as they re-live their childhood, for Lynda and Christine is that the surviving brother Arthur, living and working still, as an artist in Durban is too far away to have made the trip for the filming. Originally trained as a pilot in the RAF Arthur Morris fell in love with South Africa when posted there during World War II and decided to stay.

Despite losing three members of her close family in such a brief span of time, Emma Morris' loving legacy was happy, stable children who grew into happy, stable and loving adults. She would have regarded that as a successful achievement, they do.

Helena and Kristina Baker's other grandmother is Angela Baker, whose grandfather William Clarke, was born in Worsborough Bridge, so like virtually every other young male in the district he worked at Barrow pit. It was automatic if your father worked there he got you a job there, and you followed him down the pit. That way there was security in the family income when the inevitable illness or injury struck down the main breadwinner. Rippers were the earners on the coalface, trained, still powerfully strong, young men who could attack a coalface with a pick and shovel for eight hours and still crawl back through thirty inch high tunnels to the cage at the end of the shift as fast as anybody else. Big hitters in every sense, they earned more money than the rest and that, combined with their youth and strength gave them the respect, admiration and envy of the whole community.

Others gained it by working their way into management, like William Clarke. He lived across from the pit in Park Row and as under manager could afford a two-week holiday every summer. There were many who never left the downwardly spiralling work of hewer or ripper until their health, lungs or knees, were destroyed by the work, that had once to their young eyes looked like easy living. To the less able or physically worn out, poorly paid on unproductive 'button jobs', an annual holiday was a dream. They saved and contributed all year to ensure their kids had a place on the club or colliery social clubs' day out to the seaside.

But there was no differentiation between management and men when the cage broke and fell to the bottom of the shaft. An early recollection of William's son Frank, was of his Dad joining the men in the rescue operation and the appalling memories it left with him for the rest of his life. Like my own father and his brothers Charlie, Frederick, Eric and Kenneth in 1936 following the explosion at Carlton Pit, they collected fragmented bodies trying to piece together arms and legs to carry, blanket-covered and horror-hidden, past the fearful waiting families on the pit top. Then at fifty-one years of age there were for him no more tram rides from Barnsley to the bottom of Worsboro' Bridge with a last gasping walk up to Park Terrace. William Clarke died of silicosis, which like leukaemia, is no respecter of persons.

His son Frank would not share that fate. His mother Lucy Annie was born a Broadhead in Stocksbridge some nine miles or so away. She was the only girl in a family of eleven children and the daughter of the local butcher. Anyone living on the Stocksbridge side of Barnsley will tell you still that Broadhead's pork pies and sausages were the best in the world. Slightly further south or east there is no doubt in anyone's mind that the accolade rightly belongs in Barnsley itself where Albert Hirst was regularly, and rightly also named as world champion black pudding maker.

Frank went to work as an apprentice for Broadheads. If sleeping on a straw mattress on the floor of a single candle-lit attic above the shop with a cold water tap in the yard for washing, is a softer option, then it was. The fourteen hour day often left the thirteen year old Frank too tired to make comparisons. Life gradually improved together with his prospects and Frank married his ATS sweetheart Joyce when they had saved up enough clothing coupons for their outfits, ration food coupons for the 'do' and money for the cost of the wedding, with a honeymoon in Scarborough. After the war, with Frank now successfully running the butchering business and Joyce out of the services, daughter Angela was born.

Loved, wanted and totally secure little Angela Clarke was, she claims every bit as big a show off as Lynda Logan. She would happily perform at the Sunday School Anniversary, if picked, but like the rest had little or no idea what *The Anniversary* actually was, but believes now that these early performances were the cornerstone of her subsequent ability to perform publicly. She sang with Sunday School in Christmas sing-songs at the local pub, attended the local Friday night Youth Club and joined all the activities there, including the popular bike-rides and bilberry-picking. There was, as she recalls, always something to do, the word bored had not yet been invented it seemed.

Life was semi-rural, easy and trouble-free. She would go, with her father, to Penistone Market to buy pigs, often having the runt of a litter as a special pet. The others she played with as dolls. She helped in the shop, even watching and later helping with the blood-catching in the slaughterhouse. Bizarre by today's standards maybe, but an apt training ground for her subsequent move to the farming community of the Dales. She remembers too watching the Coronation in 1953 like half the population of the UK, on somebody else's telly. A nine-inch black and white TV with a magnifying glass in front would not suffice for most children's bedroom viewing now, but then it was a luxury. And of course there was school every day, no-one had a day off then.

The 1940s and 1950s education system in Barnsley allowed wide and sound provision flawed only by occasional individual practice. Academic creaming and streaming following the *1944 Education Act* allowed local children county minor scholarships to the town's boys' Grammar and girls' High Schools. Those not achieving the required standard in the 11 plus examination were allocated places in Central Schools with a possibility of subsequent transfer to the High or Grammar school if evidence of late development warranted it. Further provision in Secondary Modern Schools catered for those children deemed unlikely to benefit from the more academic emphasis of the other schools. These children were in my view failures only of the system not failures themselves, as so many have gone on to prove.

At age fourteen many of the children in central and secondary schools transferred to what they regarded as more desirable courses, at the Town's Mining and Technical College. Here a wide selection of electrical, technical and mechanical engineering training compensated for any earlier shortcomings. The locally relevant training was effective and highly

Dr Bernard Walkden. *Bernice Wilkinson's collection*

regarded in providing boys with suitable qualifications and a future in the area's ever-expanding mining industry.

Equally highly regarded was the Commerce and Business course taken predominantly by girls. In 1945, hot on the heels of the new education legislation, Barnsley was fortunate in appointing one Bernard Walkden as new Head of the Department of Commerce and Education. His route to the town was somewhat circuitous, but that very fact was to provide a range of experience and vision that would raise the course, and ultimately the College, to a new level of success of which Angela Clarke became part.

Bernard Walkden qualified as a Chartered Accountant and carried on a successful practice in the textile town of Radcliff, Lancashire in the 1930s, and gained a degree in Commerce at Birmingham University in 1939. He was then seconded to the Ministry of Supply where, as assistant to Sir Henry Benson he investigated the awarding of contracts and the costing of equipment for the war effort. His innate sense of purpose and tenacity are perhaps best exemplified in one element of this work which specified the need for a Spanish speaker. He was not, but learned to speak the language fluently in one year. It was possibly this ease of learning for him, that moved him to become involved in the motivation, teaching and learning achievement of others, which he surely did.

At the end of the war he moved with his wife Kathleen, son David, and daughter Bernice to Barnsley where he remained for the rest of his life. The first five years he spent re-structuring and successfully developing the department of Commerce and Education, and saw the same philosophy practically applied across the whole College enabling simultaneous curriculum expansion, and buildings extension.

Walkden's skill in combining his own philosophy and practice with the shrewd retention of those already tried and tested was one of his great strengths. He had learned in his own educational development that what an individual or situation lacked, could be provided by pragmatism or effort. Few Heads of Institutions in the middle of the twentieth century would have foreseen the vision of life-long learning that he had, fewer still would apply it to themselves as he did. Seeking to additionally strengthen his own practical experience by academic achievement, he undertook part-time research in the Department of Accountancy at the University of Sheffield gaining a PhD in the faculty of Law.

Dr Walkden was an early pioneer of partnership between Communities, Education, Commerce and Industry. His daughter Bernice Wilkinson feels he would have been delighted by the merging of these interests providing entitlement through the National Curriculum in the 1990s. His professional contributions came from a naturally easy and charming manner, which ensured his acceptance in a wide range of extra-curricular involvements. He was a Past President of the Rotary Club of Barnsley and member of the Advisory Committee for the Co-operative Retail

Society locally. At national level his inclusion, for example in membership of the Review Tribunal of Rampton Hospital, indicates his range and scope. A Directorship in the Area Health Authority has remained in the family in the form of his son-in-law Richard Wilkinson who, followed in turn by his son Nigel Wilkinson, has carried on the family tradition of accountancy to the fourth generation. Overcoming the obvious handicap of being born a Lancastrian, Bernard Walkden became, with consummate ease, a Barnsley man.

Angela Clarke had missed by a gnat's whisker being awarded a place at Penistone Grammar School which is still regarded by many locals as the best school in the district. She was therefore ready to transfer to Barnsley Mining and Technical College to undertake Bernard Walkden's two year Certificate in Commerce course. To a girl of thirteen in Stocksbridge in those days, Barnsley looked like a big city. It was an hour's journey by bus and the arrival was impressive, at the best bus station for miles.

Leaving the bus station to walk up to the College you would be struck by the unrivalled splendour of Barnsley Town Hall. Like many others Angela would sometimes walk up Regent Street imagining she was going to work in the Town Hall. Other times she would go the long route on Eldon Street, known as the Bunny Run by night, and turn right up the Arcade. Unlike many she passed Raynor's Pie shop without stopping because they did not stock Broadheads' pies, and went straight up to the top without turning into Georges Yard. The walk was a little longer but much more interesting past Olives' Gowns, Totty and Bramhams Spirella corsets, Pearls Prams and finally Guests with the wonderful aroma of fresh ground coffee on a cold day. The girls would then linger outside Hagenbachs café on Market Hill to check the menu. The height of sophistication for Angela and her friends was to dine in the upstairs café with a window table to look at the Town Hall and the College next door, infinitely better than the College provision, known to them as Swilleys.

The course Angela took included shorthand, typewriting, commerce, book-keeping, statistics, geography, English and English Literature. Incongruously, in this age of political correctness and equal opportunity, home economics was also included. On reflection she feels that this was essential in their training for the predictable role of secretary to a man who might require the occasional scone with his tea or coffee. It had its uses however. Following the massive publicity surrounding the Lady Chatterley trial, the unexpurgated version of the book was beginning to be circulated and had reached Barnsley, though not yet Stocksbridge. In great demand, a boy known only as Howard, was the first to have a copy. Trading was simple, armed with her batch of newly baked currant buns, Angela Clarke, egged on by a crowd of equally keen English Literature students, obtained and read *Lady Chatterley's Lover* aloud all the way to Stocksbridge, as Howard munched his way home in the opposite direction. She also smoked her first Park Drive cigarette on that bus, closely followed by her first experience of being violently sick, but has only happy memories of the place, the course, and the people.

Angela Clarke recalls her typing teacher as chain-smoking and sedentary. Her style was to periodically call out 'Return Carriage' from her seat at the front whilst the girls stared straight ahead, tapping keys, from which letters, numbers and punctuation marks had been removed, in automatic synchronisation to the same dreary musical accompaniment. Occasional light relief came, due to the hearing impairment of the said lady who accepted their singing as they typed in good faith. She may have not have been so accommodating had she been aware that her music had been substituted by theirs, and they were singing along to the perfectly matched rhythm of their heart-throb Elvis in his newest release, *Wooden Heart*. Whether credit was due to her teaching or Elvis is unclear, but everyone in the class passed the exam for which they were all entered. Newly qualified Miss Clarke looked back on her time there and remembered having more laughs than ever before, in days she describes as brilliant.

Angela's best friend Mary Schofield joined the Badminton Class Angela recalls, because it was run by a dishy geography teacher. Facing the prospect of an hour on the bus alone Angela bought a newspaper, and spotted an advertisement for a general clerk in the Students' Travel Office at Sheffield University. She had no hesitation in applying and no difficulty in getting the job. She shares Lynda Logan's view that life is shaped for us, as one of the very first students to come in to book a holiday was John Baker. It was love at first sight, as he went in for a holiday and came out with his future wife. The couple's wedding in Stocksbridge was carefully timed to avoid having the bus queue of workers from Samuel Fox's factory lined up behind the happy couple on the wedding photographs.

A move to live in the Dales was eased for them by Angela's early farming experiences and John's interest in becoming an environmentalist and innovator in the Yorkshire Dales National Park. His tireless work created the Hawes Countryside Museum and procurement of Millennium funding, to help secure development for the future of his beloved Dales, would have been enough of an epitaph for most people. What also remains as a testimony to him is the target of one million pounds for research into cancer which started with a joke about a nude calendar, to cheer up a man who sustained not only the Dales, but also great respect and love in the hearts of his friends.

Angela Baker survives the renewal of her bereavement, despite re-living it in such a searing spotlight as the shooting of the film brings it all back. Anyone who has suffered the loss of a loved one awaiting the inevitable outcome of the diagnosis, knows it is virtually impossible even to smile. In the dark days waiting for the worst to happen, John Baker would listen and look at Terry Logan for confirmation that it really was all happening as the girls tried to raise his and Angela's spirits by talking about the calendar. They envisaged the day it would be on sale in the village post office as disbelieving locals went in to collect their pensions, or buy their Christmas stamps. Realising their nudity might be displayed and sold as far afield as Skipton left them rocking with laughter, as they realised they could never again shop, bank or visit a dentist without the risk of some complete stranger recognising them, and internally visualising their boobs or bums. Angela Clarke had come a long way with Lady Chatterley on the circular route of the Stocksbridge bus.

Now it is Julie Walters who is playing her on screen, and Angela smiles for publicity shots with her as if she has done it every day of her life. She glances round for the approving eye of her son Matthew and daughter Rachel, taking strength from them. They are portrayed by local people in the film, and find it strange to watch an interpretation of their own story developing through the machinery of the slick professionalism that we stand and observe. Angela combines chatting to people she knows and smilingly signing autographs for people she doesn't know, but is really acting now because you can hardly tell how much she wishes John Baker was standing there with her. She does not for one minute believe that her loss is greater or more worth the telling

John Baker, before his illness, with daughter Rachel's children, Emma and Harry. *Angela Baker's collection*

Tricia Stewart with Helen Mirren, Angela Baker, Julie Walters (and Matthew Baker) in costume for the film. *The author*

than anyone else's. She is still too much of a Barnsley lass for 'side' like that.

She watches her father, Frank, return a wave from John Alderton who plays John Baker in the film, and then walk back to his position for a retake. As the call, 'Background Action' sets Frank off again walking across camera in his part as an extra she smiles and shakes her head in amused disbelief. She knows full well that soon, someone will sit in a cinema somewhere near Barnsley, and say, 'Hey look at him, he's the spitting image of that butcher from Stocksbridge where we used to get our pork pies!'

All six take it in their stride even though the demands on their time have changed their lives beyond recognition, since that impromptu start to what has become one of the most famous and successful fund raising initiatives ever. It is quite an experience to sit with these, ordinary women and talk about their extraordinary experiences. Distinctly independent yet united, their favourite memories of people and occasions vary as widely as their personalities, strengths and contributions.

The sagely deceptive Miss January was accustomed to taking the chair as President of Rylstone Women's Institute. Another seat on coast-to-coast US TV show *Tonight* gave her the opportunity to meet its host Jay Leno, her personal favourite celebrity. It was his way of wrapping his wit

Former Stocksbridge to Barnsley bus traveller Angela Baker now flies high and returns from a helicopter trip round the statue of Christ the Redeemer in Rio de Janeiro. *The author*

in patience and kindness that impressed her most, making a pleasure out of what could so easily have been a pressure. She felt he had a real and personal feel for fund-raising which came through, making the experience so enjoyable. The fact that when they met Michael Palin, he told them that he could not get on the programme, made it seem all the more unbelievable. She ranked it as big a memory as being serenaded on the *Royal Variety Show* by Peter Skellern and Richard Stilgoe with a song written specially for them. Not for Kylie, not for Jayne McDonald, nor Jane Horrocks, nor even for Shirley Bassey who were all on the same show – but for them, the Calendar Girls.

A giggling Miss February sat in a different chair to meet her favourite celebrity when she was invited by Michael Parkinson to join him on stage from her place in the audience of his TV show. She sat next to him in the blue chair where so many legendary guests have sat when appearing on the BBC's *Parkinson* show. He held her hand and told his audience that the two had a lot in common and had to stick together since they both came from Barnsley, and both went to school there.

There is another occasion which is at the top of her list of unbelievable experiences and meetings. One afternoon towards the end of filming, wine-fortified, she invited all the cast to afternoon tea, thinking she

Assistant Director Lee escorts Julie Walters to her starting point for the next scene. *The author*

Photographer of the original calendar, Terry Logan with Matthew Baker and his mother Angela and other calendar girls and stars. *The author*

John Alderton, with shaved head, sheltered from the sun by an autograph hunter. *The author*

A rare sight – a fully dressed Baker's Half Dozen in their characters' clothes, first morning of filming. *The author*

would impress them with home-made scones. It had seemed a good idea until she found herself in total panic, waiting for them all to arrive. Julie Walters, Celia Imrie, Linda Bissett, Helen Mirren, John Alderton, and Director Nigel Cole. Together with Voice Coach Andrew Jack, as dishy as any geography teacher, and recently returned from New Zealand having completed work on *Lord of the Rings*, there they were, all sitting round her kitchen table eating her scones. Now she saw the real purpose of the home economics element in Dr Walkden's curriculum.

For Miss July, who it has to be said, does seem to have something of the siren in her, the man and the moment were together at the *Dominion Theatre*, following the *Royal Variety Show*. Waiting in line to be presented to Prince Charles she alleges she saw Lionel Richie wink at her. Now claiming it was solely because of this action on his part that she felt obliged to go over to speak to him, and innocently thank him for the many hours of pleasure he had given her over the years. She further claims that she was then taken completely by surprise when he responded by kissing her. She is the one who looks most aloof on the calendar, but what you see is not always what you get, and maybe that is what Prince Charles spotted.

Angela Baker and Michael Parkinson sticking together. *Angela Baker's collection*

It is however, exactly what you get with Miss October, spontaneously remembering the utter elation she felt when she first saw her calendar picture on the front cover of her own book, on sale in Hatchards next door to Fortnums and Masons. Having kept in almost daily email contact with her daughter Lizzi who was in Australia, meant the story was virtually written. My belief is that it was the book itself that decided Helen Mirren to play the part of Tricia Stewart in the film. Outside Scandinavia I know few people who, in mind or body, are capable of greater bare-cheeked honesty than this woman, whose idea started off the whole remarkable adventure.

Miss September's favourite person was the thinking-woman's toyboy, Ian Hislop. Initially wary of the sharp wit she had enjoyed on *Have I Got News For You*, she was instantly disarmed by his ease of friendliness and approachability, on meeting him at The Oldies Award Ceremony at Simpsons on the Strand. She found him fascinating and herself fluttering. Her event to be remembered was The Women of the Year Lunch, which she loved. Commered by the bright and clever Floella Benjamin the event for her was a riot of success, talent, high fliers and glamour, as big a buzz as The Woman's Journal Fashion Show. Despite her college based day job involving daily contact with Art, Design and Fashion links she left the catwalk on that day – with a lump in her throat and tears in her eyes.

Miss November felt very differently. Possibly more shy than the others, certainly the shortest, she was chosen to lead the girls out onto the catwalk

Julie Walters with Angela Baker and her friend Christine Caston who was an extra in the film. *The author*

and was absolutely terrified by the prospect. This woman, who throughout the photographic sessions for the calendar had steadfastly refused to remove her underwear, stood shaking back-stage as the sound of Hot Chocolate's opening bars cued her entrance. She did believe in miracles as she walked into the limelight, to a reception that made her feel she was a five feet ten, slender, sensual, svelte, sophisticated, slinky, smooth and sexy thing. The crowd of women who had paid £50 per head for their tickets went mad, and she had never felt so good in her entire life. Possibly that was the first time anybody saw the real Ros fully revealed. It did not last long however, when introduced to Peter O'Toole, the best chat-up line she could think of for her long-time heart-throb was to offer to knit him a scarf.

Just as there are thirteen in a Baker's Dozen, in this Baker's Half Dozen there are seven. Terry Logan is the seventh, the man behind the lens, the man behind the scenes. Watching the magical bringing together of talent

Ros Fawcett met her long-time film favourite, Peter O'Toole and made him an offer. *Ros Fawcett collection*

and technology that make the film happen, gave him the greatest buzz. It was he says, like seeing a painting coming together. He thinks he might have fallen in love again, this time with Helen Mirren. He found her 'just so nice as well as beautiful and clever,' and could not believe she was standing with him in deep conversation about the lighting or the photography day after day.

He is not portrayed as himself in the film. His involvement is provided instead by a fictional character. That is irony if you ever heard the Logan's recount the story of Lord Lichfield being interviewed by Don McClean on *Good Morning Sunday* at the time of the original calendar. Praising the wonderful lighting of the photographer his Lordship they claim, remarked that he had photographed the famous Pirelli calendars with beautiful live models and done no better than Terry Logan, (considering what he had to work with!) You can't follow that Logan says and then he did, recreating the quality of the original calendar in the sepia subtlety of the new Baker's Half Dozen Collectible card. And yet again with a brand new Calendar for 2004 Terry Logan has photographed the original six nudes to join Buena Vista's Helen Mirren, Julie Walters, Celia Imrie, Penelope Wilton, Linda Bissett, and Annette Crosbie.

These people move in and out of the spotlight and yield the floor with professional ease. There is no evidence of jockeying for position, the politics of empire-building, envy or one-up-manship do not exist

The other side of the camera for Terry Logan. Aged nine months. *Terry Logan's collection*

in their philosophy, only one and all for the cause. In return for donations to the charity they sign cards as we talk seeming neither to realise or mind how much of themselves they continue to give to this cause. Diverse but indivisible they are six of the best, they will raise that million pounds and two of them are from Barnsley. Two out of six isn't bad either, Stan.

Final Acknowledgements

There is clearly a need for a further volume, or more, to celebrate other areas and achievements of characters who equally merit inclusion, but space has not allowed it.

The endeavours of all of the contributors have enhanced the image and reputation of Barnsley, the town I live in. Without their willingness to sacrifice some of their privacy, it would not have been possible to provide these examples of role modelling for local, national and international success. For their generosity and co-operation, in making time to share their experience, and their stories, I am most grateful. My thanks, equally, are due to the families of Ronnie and Ricki Dukes, Sir Thomas Elmhirst, George Porter, Alice Robinson and Bernard Walkden for materials, memories and support.

I am particularly grateful to the following professionals for their kindness in giving permission for their photographic and artistic work to be reproduced in this book. John Britton, CHALK PR, Patrick Eagar, Emmerdale Press Office Yorkshire Television, Tony Heald, Terry Logan, Stephen McClarence, Mike Swallow, Simon Rae-Scott and J & K Wood Gallery.

Barnsley community solicitors, Raleys, have been generously supportive in sponsoring the launch of this book, together with Brooklands Hotel and Pollyanna.

The following people have also made contributions in a number of ways for which I thank them all. Their creative ideas, constructive criticism, professional advice, physical support, mechanical assistance, photographs, paintings, encouragement and hospitality have enabled me to complete a lengthy and sometimes demanding, but mostly enjoyable and fascinating task.

Nick Balac, Connie Barstow, Rodney Bickerstaffe, Doris Blackburn, Ron Blackburn, Norman Booth, Arthur Bower, Anne Bradwell, John Britton, Mark Britton, Jason Brook, Pat Brook, Sir Colin Budd, Linda Burgess, Averil Cameron, Belle Cannan, Tony Capstick, Sven Christensen, Mick Clapham, Christine Clarke, Frank Clarke, Ian Clayton, Dick Clegg, Aileen Cook, Barry Cook, Brian Dale, Margaret Dale, Phil Davies, Maria Dukes, Perry Dukes, Eileen Ellis, Jonathan Ellis, Keith Ellis, Jennifer Elmhirst, Richard Elmhirst, Marjorie Exley, Anita Fisher, David Frances, Joyce Fruin, June Gill, John Godber, Gloria Goldsborough, Trevor Goldsborough, Colin Goulding, George Gregg, Geoff Grundy, Gloria Gunson, Ken Hall, Francis Hamilton, Muriel Hampshire, Kevin Harris, Gordon Hinchliffe, Marion Hodge, Dorothy Hyman, Eric Illsley, Andrew Jack, Eric Jackson, Heather Jackson,

Geraldine James, Paul Lafferty, Brian Lock, Sybil Maley, Lady Mason, Dame Helen Mirren, Gary Moore, Arthur Morris, Margaret Mosley, Terry Mullen, Josie Muxlow, May North, Kevin Oakes, David Oddie, Tony Peel, Emily Penn, Tom Pickering, Glyn Robinson, Margaret Sanders, Anne Sanderson, Julie Saunders, Alan Scotthorne, Richard Scudamore, Jeanette Short, Pam Stimpson, Katharine Sunderland, Linda Sutcliffe, Mike Swallow, Mavis Taylor, David Topliss, Daryl Topliss, Julie Walters, Denis White, Bernice Wilkinson, Dick Wilkinson, Kathleen Wilkinson, Mark Wilkinson, Marc Winer, Maureen Wood, Maureen Young, and Alan the coach driver who I am sure would not have missed anyone along the way. If I have, I offer my sincere apologies to them.